Ndito Akwa Ibom and A True Nigerian Man & Woman

All rights reserved
Copyright © Solomon ETE, 2008
Solomon ETE is hereby identified as author of this work in accordance with Section 77 of the Copyright, Designs and Patents Act 1988

The book cover picture is copyright to Solomon ETE

This book is published by
King Solomon Spiritual Library
P O BOX 27394
London E12 6WW UK
www.kingsolomonspirituallibrary.com
www.ksslibrary.com
ksslibrary@yahoo.co.k
This book is sold subject to the conditions that it shall not, by way of trade or otherwise, be lent, resold, hired out or otherwise circulated without the author's or publisher's prior consent in any form of binding or cover other than that in which it is published and without a similar condition including this condition being imposed on the subsequent purchaser.

A CIP record for this book is available from the British Library
ISBN 978-0-9561498-1-7

Contents

PART ONE 5-53
AKWA ABASI IBOM ETE

PART TWO 55-91
A TRUE NIGERIAN MAN AND WOMAN

PART THREE 93-135
FORERUNNER

PART FOUR 137-169
THE CHARACTER OF THE UNIVERSAL NEW WORLD

PART FIVE 170-181
THE VOICE OF THE CREATOR

PART SIX 183-219
THE INSPIRATIONAL WRITERS

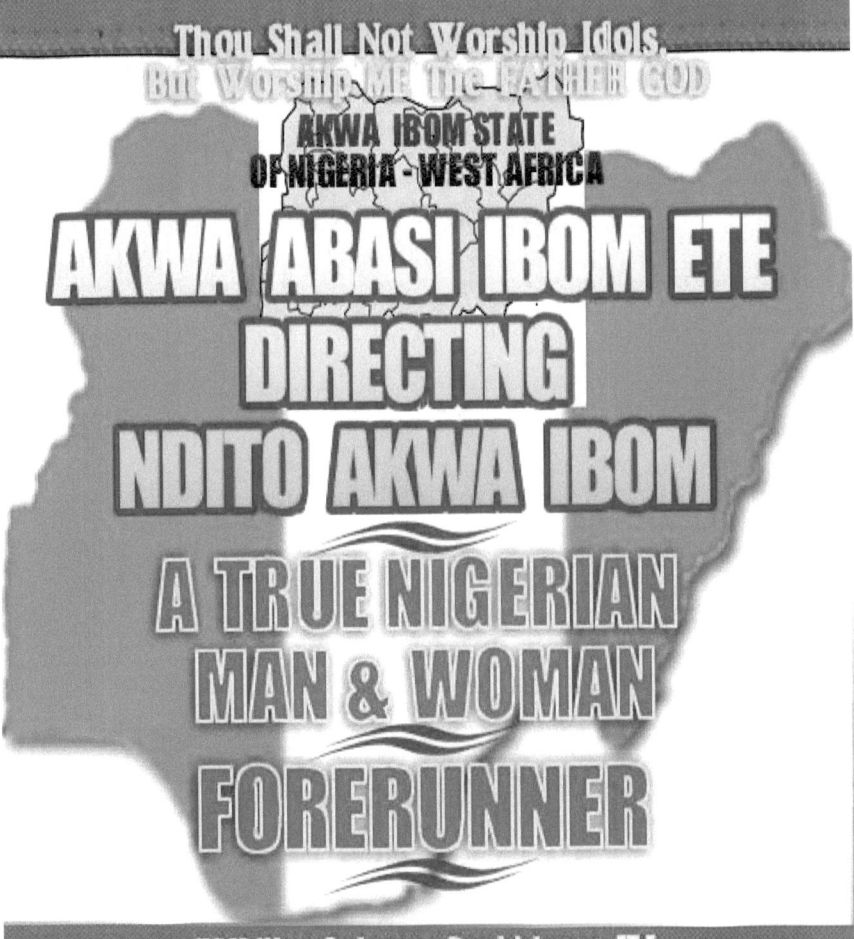

Ndito Akwa Ibom and A True Nigerian Man & Woman

KING SOLOMON SPIRITUAL LIBRARY THE GOD ENCYCLOPAEDIA WORD OF INFINITY

BY
THE SPIRIT OF THE FATHER
GOD
THROUGH HIS SERVANT
HRM KING SOLOMON DAVID JESSE ETE
(King Solomon Spiritual Library)
Eteroyal Universal Family - BCS

CHAPTER ONE

AKWA ABASI IBOM ETE DIRECTING NDITO AKWA IBOM

FATHER'S TALK
(GOD PRESENT)

Date: Christ Our Lord Thirtieth Philip, **FATHER** Two Thousand and Eight (CO.OH.BOOH) Saturday Thirtieth August Year two Thousand and Eight (30.08.2008)

In the Name of Our Lord Jesus Christ, In the Blood of Our Lord Jesus Christ, Now and forever more

Today! It pleases **ME THE FATHER GOD THE CREATOR OF THE UNIVERSE** to give this Lecture Revelation titled, **AKWA ABASI IBOM ETE DIRECTING NDITO AKWA IBOM.**

INTRODUCTION

This Lecture Revelation is about **NDITO AKWA IBOM STATE OF NIGERIA.** It does not really mean only those who live there or the indigenes or those who are born there. It means there is a seed of the plantation that germinated and I took it and planted it in that centre of a place from the origin of time.

Since I have given the Lecture Revelation from the archives records about *THE NIGERIA IN AFRICA,* I have to talk about **Akwa Ibom State,** the birth State of HRM King Solomon David Jesse **ETE** and the transit area of the children of Israel's last bus stop. They moved to Egypt and from Egypt to Ethiopia and then moved to all parts of Africa, but when they came to South West and East of the ocean where they could not pass through, they stopped there. And that was where everything ended, as that was where it all started in the beginning.

I, THE FATHER GOD is the only **ONE** that knows this information because I kept the record with **MYSELF** and this is the time to bring it out. Most of these things have nothing to do with academia and they have nothing to do with history as presented in this world. Who can give the history of time and of the whole universe? I **AM** The HISTORY **MYSELF.** When you were not somewhere when something happened then how can you say what you did not see? And how can you speak what you did not hear? You should therefore, know that **THE FATHER GOD** is the only history keeper in the King Solomon Spiritual Memory. That is why I permitted this record to be brought out.

The record you are going to hear today is not about a particular human being but about **THE FATHER GOD** and how I have programmed things. And they will begin to materialize now. From here you can do your homework and check yourself and what is happening around you. Then you will confess whether this information is a fake or it is the right information. Humble yourself, put aside the story you already have and reconcile your heart with the Spirit of **THE FATHER GOD** through this information.

Humble yourself and listen to **THE FATHER GOD** and with this humility, believe that it is only **THE SPOKEN WORD** that exists even before the physical creation. **HE** existed in **THE UNIVERSAL THOUGHT** of **THE FATHER GOD**. That **THOUGHT** is the ONE revealing this information today. The title is: **AKWA ABASI IBOM ETE DIRECTING NDITO AKWA IBOM.**

This Lecture Revelation came about today because it is the week of the Ark of the New Covenant, which I earmarked for the Renovation of the Throne of David of Israel. I promised that I would make a new covenant and that **Covenant** is **Love! Love! Love!**

I told HRM King Solomon David Jesse **ETE** to institute **The Covenant Week**, which is **The Last Seven Days Of The Month Of August Of Every Year.** And that is why today, **I AM** officially endorsing the establishment of **The Covenant Week** with this Lecture Revelation of this day, which is a revelation of the fulfilment of the promise.

A: **THE MEANING OF AKWA**

What is the meaning of **AKWA?**
AKWA means MIGHTY.
AKWA means the ALMIGHTY
AKWA means the origin
AKWA also means Adam
AKWA also means the first WORD
AKWA also means Alpha
AKWA also means the energy that starts, the starting point, the footprints.

What is the meaning of **ABASI?** You will hear that one in due course.

So, **AKWA** means **THE FATHER** that governs the existence of existing of **THE FATHER GOD,** from spirit to soul and from soul to the physical.

The Atlantic Ocean is **Akwa.**
The earth is **Akwa.**
The sky is **Akwa.**
The human system is **Akwa.**
Everything that first existed is **Akwa.**
The world itself is **Akwa.**

A to the last alphabet **Z, ZAKROLL** is **Akwa.**

If I want to give the full meaning of **Akwa** and what AKWA is attributed to like **Akwa Abasi, Akwa ETE, Akwa owo, akwa eying,** it will never end. Oldism means **Akwa.** Anything **AKWA** is the strongest of all the strongest and oldest. That is **AKWA,**

AKWA only refers to **THE FATHER GOD ALMIGHTY.** It is not the name of a group of people or any person or persons. It is not the name of any human being. It is not a human title. **AKWA** is the name of **THE FATHER GOD ALMIGHTY.**

B: THE MEANING OF ABASI

What Is the Meaning of ABASI in Efik or Ibibio language? **ABASI** means good spirit, good terms, good **GOD**. A-*Bassey edi Etii*

Abasi means anything that is fair like good business, good mind, to have a good thing as fairness treatment. **Abasi** is all blessings, all fine and all good.

Abasi is the interpretation of **GOD**.
Abasi is good.
Abasi cannot be referred as negative.
Abasi cannot be referred as Satan.
Abasi cannot be referred to be negative spirit.

Abasi can only be referred to a human-God or the Spirit of **GOD** and **THE FATHER GOD**.

Abasi refers to any good treatment, and good event. *Iso* **ABASI** for instance means the **face of GOD** or holy place of **GOD**. **Edisana ABASI**, means The Holy **GOD**. Anything you attribute to the good entity, **THE FATHER GOD** is called **ETE NNYIN ABASI**, **OUR FATHER GOD** or **ABASI ETE - GOD THE FATHER**. In another language such as Igbo or Ibo for instance,

Abasi is **Chineke.** The name in any particular language does not matter. The general reference is **GOOD GOD.** Anything that is fine and is good such as a good atmosphere, the right things, and all good things are referred to be **ABASI.**

AKWA ABASI means the **ONE** and **ONLY HIGHLY GOOD,** the phenomenon that is directing everything good. All good things came from **HIM.** That is why **HE** is referred to as **AKWA ABASI.**

C: THE MEANING OF IBOM

IBOM is not pronounced Ibómm and they do not mean the same thing. They are two different words with two different meanings.

Ibómm is *ndem* that is, the masquerade culture, which is a borrowed idea from the water realm. People cover their faces with mask and cover the rest of their body, disguising who they are. So, during the masquerade season and display the attendants and the members claiming to be the masquerades that are not humans, but spirits souls from outer space which is all farce!

Some people engage in masquerade as fun and entertainment. Some others take it so seriously. That is *Ibómm.*

IBOM means **ABASI** in adornment for the ONE and only **AKWA ABASI IBOM!** Or **IBUM ABASI 'EKA ABASI'** that signifies this is the only thing that exists in heaven and earth, that can be adorned. It means adornment! **IBOM** or **IBUM** the Glorification! The Glorious Entity! '**AKWA**' the Mighty, '**IBOM**' entity! **AKWA ABASI IBOM**, ALMIGHTY GOD ENTITY.

AKWA and **IBOM** is the ONE and the same phenomenon. **IBOM** stands for female part of **AKWA** in adornment. This is the meaning of Heaven on Earth. **AKWA** is the mental attitude of the HIGHEST AND STRONGEST GOD on the earth. It means the TOTAL ENERGY of THE FATHER GOD on earth. Heaven and Earth are **AKWA** and **IBOM,** for instant, NDITO AKWA IBOM means NDITO ETE YE NDITO EKA or NDITO EYONG YE NDITO ISONG (NDITO ABASI YE NDITO OWO), IBIBIO or IBIO-IBOM (**IBUM**) mean NDITO ISONG or NDITO OWO, You see! If you don't understand the meaning of something, you can even have that thing and joke with it.

AKWA means Heaven, First, Father, Africa, Adam, Spirit or Man, while **IBOM** means Earth, Second, Mother, Eden, Eve, Soul or Woman, (ABASI AKWA IBOM) ABASI EYONG YE ISONG, GOD OF HEAVEN AND EARTH, MIGHTY GOD ON EARTH (ADAM AND EVE) IN AFRICA. And that is that Almighty of everything cannot only be on earth. **HE** must come from *Intermodom* that is, from *Higheristy* to *midleristy* and *domeristy.*

Higheristy is the Highest of highest. *Midleristy* is here around you. And then *Domeristy* is beyond you.

That is why EVERYWHERE is **AKWA**, HERE is **ABASI** and THERE is IBOM, and that is Heaven, Earth and Hades. That is why we have **AKWA ABASI IBOM** and all is in one **SUPREME SPIRIT** of **AKWA ABASI ETE, ALMIGHTY FATHER GOD.**

D: **THE MEANING OF ETE**

What Is The Meaning Of ETE? Ettéh is the English pronunciation of **ETE**. **ETE** means **Father**. What is the meaning of **THE**

FATHER? *HE IS THE FATHER.* Who is THE FATHER? *HE IS THE SPIRIT "AKWA"* and I projected **MYSELF** 'AKWA into **ABASI**.

ABASI means the **WORD** that **I THE FATHER GOD** used for doing creations. **AKWA** means the all starting self as the only phenomenon that is The **BEGINNING**. **IBOM** means the GOD of NATURAL physical creations that exist on earth and two are Heaven on Earth. Who is the middle ONE? The middle one is, **ABASI, THE WORD "IKO"** which means **ABASI**, THE SPIRIT OF THE **WORD**.

THE SPOKEN WORD is *Iko Abasi.* The **WORD** is **ABASI**. In the beginning was the WORD and the WORD was **GOD** and the WORD was with **GOD**. This WORD is **GOD "ABASI"**. What is **ABASI? HE** is GOOD. What is GOOD? *HE IS THE SPIRIT* that is good. And all these phenomenal entities come from whom? They all come from **ME 'ETE'** that is, **FATHER - THE FATHER GOD THE CREATOR,** The Owner Of All Things, The All and All, The Head of ALLTHINGS Brotherhood, **THE TOTALITY OF TOTALITIES.**

What are you going to argue about this? Bring your own version, if you think you know more than what **I THE FATHER GOD** knows. You read the bible. You read stories. People would say, 'Oh this **FATHER'S TALK (GOD PRESENT)** Lectures Revelations do not have quotations from the Holy Bible.

Who is the Bible? The **WORD** is the Bible. When the people that spoke the words of the Bible were speaking then that resulted in the writing of the Bible and whom did they quote? They quoted **THE FATHER GOD** so it is **THE FATHER GOD** that is talking now therefore, **AM I** not greater than the Bible?

Use the WORD of **THE FATHER'S TALK (GOD PRESENT)** to compare with the Bible. Then you will come to know that this **FATHER'S TALK (GOD PRESENT)** is the one that gave birth to the Bible in the first place. Therefore, **I AM** NOT quoting Isaac. **I AM** NOT quoting Jeremiah. **I AM** not quoting anybody because before Abraham I was. **I AM** quoting **MYSELF** the **WORD** who is ALL AND ALL, **THE FATHER'S TALK (GOD PRESENT)**.

I THE FATHER GOD I AM the **"ETE"**, The Origin Of Everything. **HE IS THE SPIRIT,** Unhearable, unseen-able and untouchable that became hearable, seen-able and touchable. So **ETE** is **HE IS THE FATHER.** When you hear this Revelation Lecture, then you must rearrange yourself and your thoughts from today.

I WANT THIS LECTURE REVELATION TRANSCRIBED, PROOFREAD AND PRODUCED IMMEDIATELY AND GIVEN TO ALL INDIGENES OF THE WHOLE WORLD, ESPECIALLY THOSE OF **AKWA IBOM STATE OF NIGERIA.**

I want them to know that **THE AKWA IBOM STATE** children of **THE FATHER GOD** should be DIRECTED BY **THE HOLY SPIRIT, THE FATHER GOD**, since they are **NDITO AKWA ABASI IBOM.**

If anyone with any negative instinct, negative behaviour with an evil spirit in them takes birth and is born there, I will send the person(s) back to where such individual or individuals came from in nature.

The remnants of **MY** children that will stay are the ones from **ME.** They are from the original template of Abel the positive part of Adam. They will stay with **ME** in the world without end. I have come to renovate that place and establish **MY** peaceful Kingdom of **GOD** there to set an example of equality of treatment, good roads, free transportation, free amenities including water, electricity and many others. I have put enough wealth in **AKWA IBOM** that can feed the whole Nigeria, even the whole of Africa, and indeed the whole world.

IF ANYBODY BECOMES JEALOUS ABOUT THIS LECTURE REVELATION OF **AKWA IBOM** AND PLANS EVIL, I WILL RETURN THAT PERSON'S SOUL OF NATURE TO WHERE I TOOK HIS OR HER NATURE OF CREATION FROM AND THEY WILL NEVER FOREVER TAKE BIRTH AGAIN HERE. SO, WHEREVER ANYBODY IS REMEMBER THIS!

THE FATHER GOD IS THE SUPREME WORD and the WORD is everything. All **AKWA IBOM** children from spiritual origin should rejoice because there shall be no more "ISO EKPO, ISO ASAN, ISO IBOK, ISO NDEM, ISO MBIAM", and there shall be no more, "EKPO NYOHO OR EKPO

EKONG, NDEM EFIK, NDEM IBIBIO, ATAT, EKONG, OBON, AND ANY TRADITIONS THAT IS NOT FROM **ME THE FATHER GOD** IN AKWA IBOM STATE OR EVEN IN THE ENTIRE OF NIGERIA. ALL AKWA ABASI IBOM CHILDREN IN NIGERIA SHOULD TRY ALL POSSIBLE MEANS TO SHOW THEIR IDENTITY AS THE POSITIVE TRUE CHILDREN OF THE FATHER GOD ON EARTH, BECAUSE YOU ARE THE BLESSED NATION AND THE BLESSED PEOPLE. Even if you are from somewhere else or manifested physically anywhere else, but you are lucky to have a connection with **AKWA IBOM** in anyway, you should count yourself lucky. Make merry! Celebrate about this Revelation Lecture. Believe in your heart and have evolution from today that you are a blessed sanctuary of **THE FATHER GOD** and that you came from the soil of blessing and that I have revealed you and you must reveal yourself in all good manners of positivism.

If you are into secret society practices, if you practice evil, if you are involved in witchcraft and practice or have evil spirit of hatred and destroy people's life, kill people, then you will have your verdict from this year upwards. And whatsoever you see don't doubt.

In **AKWA IBOM STATE** particularly and in Nigeria specifically and Africa as a whole, no one or group or state should go into battle of war with another person or group or state anywhere.

No one should fight with a fellow human being.

No human being should kill another human being.

Nobody should plan to kill or perform any evil to another human being, in the physical or spiritual way.

No negativism should operate in all the EFIK, AND IBIBIO or OBIO AKPAN ABASI (BIAKPAN) and entire of country NIGERIA, AFRICA AND ENTIRE WHOLE WORLD.

Everyone should be natural and live with positive love, peace, unity and oneness with the practice of equal opportunity for the better quality of life with all humankinds.

And I bless all of you! I will stand behind you to exhibit the Nature of **THE FATHER GOD** in the land of AKWA ABASI IBOM.

The whole world will come there to share with the blessing. They will equally bring their own blessing and share with your blessing. **I AM** starting now with ONE COMMON PURSE, which will consist of **Give Me I Give You** and **Love me I love you.** Serve **THE FATHER GOD** with love, with humility and with oneness of everything.

AKWA IBOM STATE children of **THE FATHER GOD** should set example for other people on earth. Give them peace because HRM King Solomon David **ETE** originally as Abel manifested in **AKWA IBOM** and that means PEACE manifested in that whole area physically. So, you should start that peace. Start using the energy of peace now and save the whole world.

On wealth, everybody knows that wherever HRM King Solomon is born there is always wealth. There is enough physical and spiritual wealth. And there is power of spirit so you only have to believe and then tap it. You should also know that you have freewill because what belongs to **THE FATHER GOD** belongs to the positive children of **THE FATHER GOD** and what belongs to the children belongs to **THE FATHER GOD.**

When I say **AKWA IBOM**, I don't just mean that particular corner of that State, I mean Nigeria as whole. I mean the whole of Africa. I mean the whole world. **I AM AKWA ABASI IBOM ETE THE UNIVERSAL FATHER GOD.** That is the meaning of that.

The point and the spot do not matter, but it is the SPIRIT, which matters, which is The Holy Spirit of Truth lavishly covers the entire universe. So, when you read the Revelation Lectures titled, *NIGERIA IN AFRICA, THE TRUE NIGERIAN MAN AND WOMAN* and then you read this **AKWA ABASI IBOM ETE DIRECTING NDITO AKWA IBOM,** you will know what **I AM** talking about.

ETE means **THE FATHER GOD ALMIGHTY.**

ETE also means **GOD THE FATHER** on earth.

And **ETE** also means **Abasi – IKO ABASI ETE.**

I gave a Lecture Revelation about *GOD THE FATHER, GOD,* and *THE FATHER*

GOD ALMIGHTY. All are the same entity in meaning, but serve different roles. **GOD THE FATHER** is the **Father** of all human beings on earth, '**AKPA OWO**' '**AKWA OWO**' or '**JESSE**' **THE ROOT OF ALL MEN OR JESS-US - ALL MEN**, who was Adam and also Adam today and will be the same new **ADAM** tomorrow. He is the head of all human beings, the first energy of all human beings, where **THE SUPREME WORD** first materialized as a human being.

And whenever **THE SUPREME WORD** becomes a human being and takes the capacity of that total **WORD** in that person, such a person becomes **GOD THE FATHER** on earth.

Then **GOD** is the **WORD HIMSELF.** This is **THE SPOKEN WORD,** the spirit-soul of **THE FATHER GOD** and that is the middle **Entity**. **GOD HIMSELF** is that.

HE can be a servant.

HE can be a Spirit Soul.

He can be anything.

I can call **MYSELF** The Son, but **I AM Emmanuel,** which means **GOD,** is with mankind. Then **I THE FATHER GOD, I AM** *HE IS THE SPIRIT*, **THE MAKER OF ALL THINGS, AND THE SUPREME THOUGHT**

OF ALL CREATION. I AM THE SPIRIT Unhearable; unseenable and untouchable that is, cannot be heard, cannot be seen and cannot be touched but I became heard-able, seen-able and touchable. That is the meaning of **GOD THE FATHER, GOD** and **THE FATHER GOD.**

When you read the full Lecture Revelation I gave about this, you will not be confused again by thinking that **GOD** is three. However, as I said earlier, the three phenomenon's are, **THE SPIRIT**, the **NAME** of the Spirit that manifested and the **BODY** (container) that **THE SPIRIT** took. So you have the **Product**, the **Container** and the **Label**. That is why human being is God. So, do not be stupid and become *idiotikot* by refusing to understand the truth because when you betray the truth, you are in trouble.

E: **THE DIRECTING FORCE**

What is **The Directing Force That Will Direct All Ndito Akwa Ibom** that is, all children of **THE FATHER GOD** and all positive human beings on earth? **The**

Directing Force is The Holy Spirit, the Truth - The Holy Spirit of Truth.

The Holy Spirit of Truth is the phenomenon you cannot bribe. Generally people talk about the connections of places such as the Calabar area, Akwa Ibom, Biakpan, Arochukwu, Benin, Asaba and the Delta area and so on.

Do you see the water that runs through the middle of Nigeria called the Niger Delta River? I revealed this before that there is a secret behind it in the creation by **THE FATHER GOD** from the beginning of time in the land of Africa.

THE CREATING FORCE OF THE FATHER GOD buried great power and a lot of good things in Nigeria, Ghana and many other numerous places in the whole of Africa that have not yet been revealed. When the time comes, and that is when there is peace, love, unity, oneness, equality, mercy and kindness has properly established in the world, then I will bring out most of these wonderful things. I shall make the modern scientist to discover them on earth.

THERE IS SOMETHING THAT I HAVE BURIED IN THIS EARTH THAT WILL KEEP MANKIND ALIVE FOREVER AND THAT THING IS **THE TREE OF LIFE!**

I have never shown it to anybody physically yet on this earth not even an angel. And this **TREE OF LIFE IS PHYSICALLY HERE ON EARTH IN THE LAND OF AFRICA** but spiritually **THE TREE OF LIFE** is the WORD you are hearing now.

THE HOLY SPIRIT OF TRUTH PERSONIFIED IS THE TREE OF LIFE and that **HOLY SPIRIT** has manifested something as a product that will materialize, as **THE TREE OF LIFE** and when you taste that thing you will live forever. If anyone desires to have that, he or she must practice the WORD of **THE FATHER GOD**, by **SHOWING LOVE TO ME THE FATHER GOD ALMIGHTY** and all humanity.

I will not give you that access until **there is in you the indwelling spirit of unity, love, oneness, equality, kindness and peace.** Those who practice peace are the children of **THE FATHER GOD.** Blessed are the peacemakers for they shall be called the children of God. Those are the ones that wherever you see them, they are with **THE FATHER GOD** and they are the ones that will taste **The Tree Of Life.** You may even see them, but would not know they are the ones.

The Tree of Life is **THE HOLY SPIRIT** and **HE IS THE ONE DIRECTING NDITO AKWA IBOM.** In the nature, people hear about **Biakpan, Efik people, Akwa Ibom** that is, Ibibio people and Arochukwu people because they are one. Also the Yoruba and all other parts of Nigeria and Ghana to Cote D'Ivoire are all one. All Africans are one.

African people are the original human beings mixed with negative and positive. There are too many of them that are into juju evil worshipping and also the worshipping of idols, because that was what Lucifer established through the spirit of Cain on earth. Nonetheless, now **THE HOLY SPIRIT OF TRUTH** has come and established **HIS** Spiritual Kingdom of **Unity, Oneness, Equality, Kindness**, **Love, Peace** and **Righteousness,** it will superimpose all negativisms and change the entire environment of this world to be the HOME OF **THE FATHER GOD ALMIGHTY** FOR ETERNITY.

The whole world shall see the miraculous PARADISE OF **THE FATHER GOD** ON EARTH that will be established in Africa.

The Directing Forces of THE FATHER GOD in AKWA IBOM are **love, peace, mercy, kindness, joy, oneness, equality, unity** and all the rest of the characteristics of **THE FATHER GOD**. When you have all these characters in you then **I AM** directing you to do what is good. The WORD of **THE FATHER GOD** that is **THE HOLY OF TRUTH** has established with PEACE in AFRICA, **AKWA IBOM, NIGERIA** and the entire **WORLD**. And there must be peace, love and unity everywhere.

All governments and especially those physically at the helm of affairs in **AKWA IBOM STATE, NIGERIA AS A WHOLE, ALL AFRICAN COUNTRIES AND THE ENTIRE WORLD** should bear in mind that **AKWA IBOM STATE, NIGERIA, ALL AFRICAN COUNTRIES, THE ENTIRE WORLD** belongs to **THE FATHER GOD ALMIGHTY** and you are in that circle of

AKWA. So, if you misuse **AKWA ABASI IBOM** amenities and **AKWA ABASI IBOM** wealth and **AKWA ABASI IBOM** treasures, you will be arrested and your life will be worse than Lucifer's life.

THIS COMES AS A **WARNING** AND AS INFORMATION TO ALL **AKWA ABASI IBOM PEOPLE IN THE ENTIRE WORLD.**

I must tell that you in future, if you want to direct, be the head of any country as in the whole of Nigeria, Ghana and indeed anywhere in Africa and the whole world or you want to occupy any prominent post, or indeed any post and position to work for **THE FATHER GOD** as a servant of **GOD** then you must use love, humility, unity, kindness, equality and peace and all the characteristics of **THE FATHER GOD** to rule. Throw away arrogance and pomposity! And don't enter into any secret evil cult or secret society! Do not use any evil means to rule **MY** children! If you do, you will be damned! Seriously! And you will become mad in spirit-soul and physical as a wanted soul in detention forever.

Use love to rule! Use **ME THE FATHER GOD ALMIGHTY, THE SPOKEN WORD** to rule! Believe that **THE CREATOR OF THE UNIVERSE, AKWA ABASI IBOM** is the **IN-CHARGE** of the whole place as the whole world and that force will be with you and nobody can do anything harmful to you! And they will see the love of **THE FATHER GOD,** the mercy of **THE FATHER GOD,** the peace of **THE FATHER GOD,** the quality of **THE FATHER GOD** flowing everywhere in the land in equal measures.

No **AKWA IBOM** indigene should lament!

No **NIGERIAN** indigene should be poor!

No **AFRICAN** child should lament!

No **GOOD CITIZEN OF THE WHOLE WORLD** should suffer and lament.

None of you should lament because of the vast amount of good things that I have buried in the whole of Africa to sustain all **MY** children. Go to Ghana for instance, and see the vast quantity of gold deposits there or is it the Diamonds in South Africa and Sierra Leone or oil and other things in Nigeria and the rest of Africa. The amount of natural resources that I have buried in Africa is enough to sustain the entire world and very, very comfortably to the extent that everyone should own a house, a car, eat well and live happily and thank **THE FATHER GOD!** Because that this is the Paradise of **THE FATHER GOD** on earth!

This is the reason **I AM** giving this message to all human beings in the entire world so that if you think that you have evil plans against this WORD, against these directives and you want to eat alone and enjoy alone then you will see yourself where you never believed to be. This WORD is not from the speaker, HRM King Solomon David Jesse **ETE**, but from THE BROADCASTING STATION OF **THE FATHER GOD, AKWA ABASI IBOM.**

Some people are stupid in their action! When they hear other peoples programs on the radio, they switch off their **radio** or tune to another channel but what they do not think about is that even when they switch to another station, the broadcasting is still going on, because they are not the broadcasting station. They are only a receiver so it would have been that they listen and inform themselves.

HRM King Solomon David Jesse **ETE** is only a receiver. He is not the broadcasting station. For that reason if you think you will not hear this message, you are telling lies. Even if HRM King Solomon David Jesse **ETE** were not able to receive and give out these numerous information's, I have many other ways and people to give **MY** information out, nonetheless, since He is able to pass on these numerous and vital information, I bless Him, and I bless **AKWA IBOM STATE.** Therefore, all children of **THE FATHER GOD** in **AKWA IBOM STATE,** the **Calabar** people, **Biakpan** and indeed the whole of Nigeria and all of Africa and the whole world should rejoice this day for THE TABERNACLE OF GOD IS WITH MAN. THE PROMISE OF **THE FATHER GOD** IS FULFILLED.

Stop condemning someone!
Stop coming into conclusion on what you don't know!
Before you comment on this **FATHER'S TALK (GOD PRESENT)** Lecture Revelation, make sure you read at least seven different titles of **THE FATHER'S TALK (GOD PRESENT)** Lecture Revelations and then you can comment. If you comment before that you may make the greatest mistake that you will not forgive

your life forever. This is the WORD of AFTER THOSE DAYS SAYS THE LORD MOST HIGH, THE TESTIMONY OF **EVERLASTING GOSPEL OF THE HOLY SPIRIT OF TRUTH PERSONIFIED ON EARTH**. That is **THE SPIRIT,** THE FORCE WHICH IS **DIRECTING NDITO AKWA ABASI IBOM.**

F: **NDITO AKWA IBOM**

Who is **Ndito Akwa Abasi Ibom? Ndito Akwa Ibom,** the true children of **Akwa Ibom** are those who have humility. In fact if you employ **Akwa Ibom** indigene or Efik person, the original "***UFAN IMA***" THE URUAN meaning DAVID the beloved in **Akwa Ibom,** *ndito Abasi*, they will stay peacefully with you and would not steal anything from you. They will not poison your food.

If you marry an Efik or Ibibio (Akwa Ibom) woman, (the positive ones) she will not betray you.

Do you know who established Calabar in the spirit soul? The spirit soul of Abraham and David was the same person in nature as our natural Father Adam. Their names as Abraham and David mean the same person, as UFAN ABASI and IMA ABASI. The same spiritual **Akwa Abasi Ibom** people are the same Calabar (Efik) people. Efik and Ibibio people are one and the same people. There is no difference between a typical **Akwa Ibom** that is Ibibio person and a typical Calabar (Efik) person or Biakpan people. A typical Ibibio, Efik and **Biakpan** are not different from one another. It is only one man and one woman that established these three places I mentioned.

Check this in **Arochukwu, Atan Anayom.** Also check this in **Abriba.** Check this in **Onah** in Igbo land. Also check this in **Asaba.** Go to **Benin** and check as well. And then cross to **Esukutan, Creek town** and cross again to **Efiatmbo.** Go to all these places and then you will see that in this **Akwa Ibom** side, in this *Ijaw* side of Rivers State, you will see why I spread **MYSELF** around. There is history, a spiritual history and miracle that I have created, which I have not revealed to any human being.

Who established the Solid Skin people (Black) of American? They were originally from Nigerian delta *Ijaw. Ijaw* wealth is the same wealth of Nigerian delta that the *Ogoni* established in the whole of America. The wealth of America came from Nigerian DELTA AND RIVER NIGER *Ijaw* through slave trade, the trading of the human beings there therefore it is the Nigerian indigenes that enriched America. That is the spiritual history as the secret behind that movement. The wealth you see in the whole world comes from the Niger Delta of **THE FATHER GOD**. It was particularly from Akwa to Abasi Ibom after the Noah Flood, when the Ijaw of Niger Delta spread to the whole world. This is the secret that I have just revealed now.

Queen Sheba's final destination was in *Ijebu Ode* in Nigeria. Queen Sheba had two natural male seeds from King Solomon descendant's spiritual incarnation soul when she finally landed in Niger Delta of Nigeria and she named that land E-JEBU (JEHOVAH GOD OF KING SOLOMON'S LOVE -IJE-BU). She no longer answered the name of the evil god SHE-BA meaning god of the EARTHLY WEALTH, but the NAME of Original FATHER GOD (EDI-BU) meaning **EDISANA ABASI** or EDISANA IKO or EDISANA BU-EKPO in changing language, '**BU**' mean Ekpo or in English Ghost or spirit soul, just like saying OBIO EKPO the city of spirit soul or ghost or you can say EBEKPO ABASI, the THRONE of GOD, EDI mean EDISANA or HOLY in the English language as HOLY SPIRIT "**EDIBU**". I will not go too much in-depth about this for now but that was where I stopped the evil not to spread again. **I AM** only pointing out these bits of information so that you know that every secret record is with **ME** and that is what I have buried in King Solomon Spiritual Library and now is the time for **THE HOLY SPIRIT** to bring them out.

THE HOLY SPIRIT is joy! Joy! Joy! So, **Ndito Akwa Abasi Ibom** are the peacemakers. If you see anyone that is not peaceful, that joined a secret society, as the people who siphon money and betray the truth, then know that such a person is not among **Ndito Akwa Abasi Ibom**. When such a person dies, he or she will not be born there again. From now on, since I have revealed the truth about this set of human beings in THE SUPREME PREMISES of **THE FATHER GOD, I AM** sending the true **Ndito Akwa Abasi Ibom** to be born there starting with immediate effect. Meanwhile, I will engineer the true ones that are already born and give them The Holy Spirit to be with **THE FATHER GOD** to change things and do what is good, and set an example of the origin of **THE FATHER GOD** to the whole world. That is how you will know and detect the true children of **THE FATHER GOD, NDITO AKWA ABASI IBOM.** They are the peacemakers. They are *ataha Nditor Akwa Ibom.*

G: ALPHA AND OMEGA RECONSTRUCTION CENTRE

AKWA ABASI IBOM means **Alpha and Omega GOD. Adam** started and **OLUMBA** ended. Put them together and they become Brotherhood, **The Centre Of Reconstruction** as the **Centre** where the whole World will come together.

Do not treat **Calabar** (Efik), **Akwa Ibom** (Ibibio) and **Biakpan** indigenes and all **African** and the entirety of humankind as though you are different from one another. You are all the same one person because it was one man that established everyone. You all have the same spiritual language of love and the same understanding of peace and unity. Whatever that brought problems to these areas and resulted in separation, I have taken it away from today, from now upward.

Ghana and Nigeria are from one Father. Nigeria and Cameroon are from one Father. The whole children of Africa are from one father Adam, so also the Arabs and the rest of the world. That being the case, wherever you are in the world, come back to be together and have peace, unity, oneness and love. Do not allow anyone to mislead you. You must use love, use peace and understanding to interact and live with one another.

What **I AM** doing now is a recreation of NDITO Akwa Abasi Ibom using this WORD of **THE HOLY SPIRIT** to upgrade the mentality of all Akwa Ibom, Nigeria, Africa and the entirety of humankind in the whole world. I upgrade the **solid-skin** or **dark-skin** humans wherever they are. I upgrade them for simplicity. I upgrade them for positive mentality to think well, to speak well, act well, do well and manage things well. I have given them the spirit of good management, to recognize one another, to love one another, to program and give what is good.

Previously, the **solid-skin** or **dark-skin** humans eat in the morning and forget about the evening. They throw things away and later go back to look for them. But from today, right from now onward the Africans, the **solid-skin** or **dark-skin** humans will have the mind to preserve things, to correct things, to rejoice with things that are good, to be happy with things that are good and to love all the things that are good, and especially to love life. Before this day they do not bother with things. The **solid-skin** or **dark-skin** humans that is, the Africans are like children who have very rich parents.

As their parents are rich, they are reluctant to go to school, because they believe their father will see to their upkeep and they will also inherit their parent's money from the will that would be made to favour them. They don't ask what their own children would eat when it becomes their turn to be the father being that they have squandered their own parents' money. That is exactly the situation with the Africans before now, but now **I THE FATHER GOD ALMIGHTY** have reversed all those attitudes.

Africans have a supply of everything in their backyard. They have fruits, vegetables herbs and so many other resources so they allowed other people to take them away and then they go back to borrow those same things others. That is not happening any no more!

From now on, I will change things for good. ***THE GREAT UNIVERSAL CHANGE*** is now in operation. You will see that from today and from now onward people will borrow from you instead of you borrowing from people. You will see that people will buy from you instead of you buying from people, people will serve you instead you being the servant to people. **I BLESS YOU THE FATHER GOD'S LAND OF AKWA ABASI IBOM! THE MOTHER'S LAND! AKWA IBOM** means Heaven and Earth. **AKWA IBOM** land means **THE FATHER** and **THE MOTHER'S** land. The whole of **AFRICA** stands for **AKWA ABASI IBOM THE BLESSED LAND**!

From today, I have blessed you! I have secured you and made all nations of the world to love you and also for you to love them and love yourselves. If anybody plans evil, then they shall die and be destroyed. If you plan evil for anybody, you will die and not come to this world again. Therefore, from today **AKWA ABASI IBOM** is talking to and directing **NDITOR AKWA IBOM.**

I have infused to you with the positive spirit of Divine love of good nature and energy of revival, to use what **I THE FATHER GOD** has given to you to salvage the whole world, now and forever more, Amen!

AKWA IBOM is the **'RECONSTRUCTION CENTRE OF AKWA ABASI IBOM ETE NNYIN DIRECTING NDITOR AKWA IBOM'** in the entire universe.

CONCLUSION A:
ONLY POSITIVISM WILL EXIST IN AKWA IBOM STATE, NIGERIA, AFRICA AND THE WHOLE WORLD

You may not like this but remember, it is only evil that does not like what is good. I know that it is only the positive people that will be jubilant and celebrate about this information. The negative people will not like it, but it does not matter.

The Father, Son and **The Holy Spirit** mean the **Word,** the **water** and the **blood** in you. And in spirit it means **I THE FATHER GOD, THE WORD** and **MAN.** Therefore, you have in you **Father, Son** and **The Holy Spirit.** If all of us stand together and vote, where will you stand to kick against **ME?** If the **Spirit** votes against the blood and water, you are finished because, The **Spirit** is **THE FATHER GOD.** That is why **HE** said; One With God Is The Majority. It is no longer the case that the majority carries the vote.

The **TRUTH** is the majority, because the **TRUTH** remains the **TRUTH** forever as it is unchangeable. So, if you think this WORD is not from **THE FATHER GOD,** then wait for **MY** due time of action, when it happens then you will know. You will start seeing **MY** Energy swap over and swallow and melt away all negativisms in the whole of **AKWA IBOM STATE,** the whole of Nigeria, Africa and the whole world. You will start seeing that judgment will start on people individually.

When you start seeing '***THE GREAT UNIVERSAL CHANGE'***, changing things around you for good for good people and for bad for bad people, then you will see that **I, AKWA ABASI IBOM ETE NNYIN** is talking.

CONCLUSION B:
CALABAR OF NIGERIA

What happened that made **ME** to establish **CALABAR OF NIGERIA. I** established Calabar of Nigeria because of the turn of events.

Calabar in Nigeria is exactly like England of the United Kingdom and **I** want to give this revelation today. There was nothing like Calabar, but there was something like ***URUAN* or *UFAN* or *IMA* of Akwa Abasi Ibom.** And there was a place like ***Arochukwu,*** *the* old city. These children of Israel moved from one place to another and they carried the African seed to plant and stayed there. This is what used to happen however, because of the worshipping of idols; I transferred the positive children of Israel that were supposed to reside in **Arochukwu** to **Ibibio** land. Ibo or Igbo people are a part of IBIBIO (NDITO IBOM). What I did was that I always changed their language to confuse them because the power of communication is from the language. The original Hebrew language, which is the original Ibibio and original Efik which was one language, is the language I spoke during creation and that is why I want to honour it.

As I always say, this STATE OF THE SPIRIT OF **ME** called **THE HOLY SPIRIT** does not accept idol worshipping and the worshiping of any gods or elementary forms. And so wherever the children of Israel moved to and saw people worshipping a strange god that is physical, which was not **THE FATHER GOD** and Adam, they would leave that place. People used to kill them and used to pursue them because whenever any of them spoke Ibibio as a spiritual natural language, the evil spirit they had there would die and that is why people used to pursue them. Finally I took them to **URUAN** in **AKWA IBOM** and that was the final stop. However because of all the same worshiping of mermaids and all the evil that started to establish in *URUAN* it led **ME** to establish **Calabar.**

Calabar was seashore, a fishing harbour of fishermen. Some of you know the story, but **I AM** not talking about the one you know. **I AM** talking about the original events as they occurred. It was an Ibibio and Ibo person that I used to establish Calabar. It was just one person of Hebrew lineage that I used to establish that place.

I established that place to be the commercial centre, as an office for **MYSELF** for when I would materialize physically. And that is where I have now established **MY** office. *Opobo* and *Igwenga* are connected to Calabar to establish the land of development that brought civilization and trade to manage the place so that the whole world should link together with Africa and this area is the centre of Nigeria, Africa and the World and now I bless the land again.

So *Igwengafrica Ikot-Abasi* and now **AKWA IBOM, (BIAKPAN) CALABAR,** and the rest of Nigeria are one. And I put a fence around them and the whole of

Nigeria. *The time shall come that there will be Twelve Major Zones and Seventy Two States in total in Nigeria, Twenty Four Local Area in each State, Seven Community Areas in each Local Area, Four Major Zones in Africa Continent to represent EAWENOSO OF THE FATHER GOD, One Hundred and Forty-Four Thousand Countries in the Whole World and a total Twelve Nations on Earth, Controlled and Managed by ME THE FATHER GOD ALMIGHTY THROUGH MY NATURAL RULERSHIP with a voted positives administrators.*

Then in **AKWA IBOM STATE** local government there will be Foremost Major Twenty-Four Local Government Authority in number that will represent Twenty-Four Elders both natural and spiritual, and **I THE FATHER, SON AND THE HOLY SPIRIT OF TRUTH**, THE SUPREME WORD OF THE UNIVERSE have already created the spiritual energy to guide and direct this arrangement. This is how **GOD** NEW ADMINISTRATION will start from here and cover the whole world as it was in the beginning world without end and so it shall be done WORD without end. And they will all be Kings and Queens. I gave HRM King Solomon David Jesse **ETE** the message about the Kings and the Queens the future's truthful chosen of **THE FATHER GOD**.

GOD ADMINISTRATION will come to correct all evils politics. It has nothing to do with churches. It has nothing to do with religions. Revelation has nothing to do with anything. It is a natural **FATHER'S TALK (GOD PRESENT)** Revelation on the ADMINISTRATION OF **THE FATHER GOD.** It accepts anybody that is positive therefore, those who are inclined to churches and those who are politically minded in evil ways can choose to accept and change their ways to positive and equality excellent dealing with all citizens. It is your choice. Nonetheless, the **Truth** remains the **Truth** forever.

Do not establish churches or any religious sects or any evil political factions.

Believe already established UNIVERSAL LOVE OF THE FAMILY OF **THE FATHER GOD,** BROTHERHOOD of the same Parent that will lead the whole world together in oneness, unity, equality, peace and love.

THE FATHER GOD is for the whole world. And **THE FATHER GOD** stands for the **TRUTH, THE HOLY SPIRIT OF TRUTH.**

LET **ME** PRESENT THIS OFFICIALLY NOW:

If you call the name of **THE FATHER GOD ALMIGHTY, THE PERSONIFIED WORD LEADER OLUMBA OLUMBA OBU** and practice witchcraft, and practice evil and do anything evil, you will be sorry for yourself because **MY Spirit** has nothing to do with anything negative. Read **THE FATHER'S TALK (GOD PRESENT)** Lecture Revelation titled, *THE TRUE LIFE OF THE HOLY SPIRIT PERSONIFIED ON EARTH*

LET **MY** PEACE AND BLESSING ABIDE WITH THE ENTIRE WORLD.

THE **CALABAR** OF NIGERIA means The Peaceful place of **THE FATHER GOD** and when you meet the true **Calabar or Ibibio** man or woman, you will be so happy because you can stay for life with them without quarrelling.

Calabar is like the United Kingdom that I established after I emigrated from the Philistines and Jerusalem and established that part of the world to create a United Nation, as a peaceful land that everybody would have access to. That is the same way I established **Calabar (BIAKPAN).** These Calabar people are the father and mother Adam. They are very, very peaceful and give a lot of cooperation. They are not aggressive people. They do not practice evil. If you meet the true Calabar person from *URUAN "UFAN" ABASI* the origin of the final positive human being, then you can assure yourself that you will be happy. That is from where I brought the awareness of positivism to this world.

CONCLUSION C:
CHILDREN OF GOD IMMIGRATION CENTRE

The Children of **GOD** immigration centre spiritually is AFRICA (EKALAND) EKARA OR EKWERE AKWA ABASI IBOM is where I migrate the children of GOD to put them in the four corners of the world, according to your original template. But you will not know this. It is a spiritual management. And it is only in this Library of **THE FATHER GOD** that you will hear this sort of information. You can never, never have it from anywhere else no matter what you conjure and any type of person you meet. And you have not heard anything yet.

I can decode and give the original information on everybody on this earth. But now, what I want is cooperation, love and peace. I will migrates all positive children of **THE FATHER GOD** and fix them where they will have happiness. So, love, peace, mercy, humility, patience, kindness, equality and oneness are what I want in the whole of Nigeria, Ghana, Cameroon, the rest of Africa and the whole world, especially in the immigration centre.

LET **MY** PEACE AND BLESSING ABIDE WITH THE ENTIRE WORLD, NOW AND FOREVER MORE. AMEN!

THANK YOU FATHER!

ENYE! ODUDU! ABASI MI! OOO! ZIM! ZIM! ZIM! ASSASSU! POSITIVE! POSITIVE! POSITIVE!

THANK YOU FATHER

Prayer by Princess Mfon Etteh to thank **THE FATHER GOD:**

*Let thanks and praises be given to **THEE FATHER** in the name of Our Lord Jesus Christ.*

*Let thanks and praises be given to **THEE FATHER** in the blood of Our Lord Jesus Christ.*

Let thanks and praises be given to Thee, now and forever more. Amen!

*Holy! Holy! Holy most loving and everlasting **FATHER,** we thank YOU and glorify YOUR name. Thank YOU **FATHER** for this wonderful day, Thank YOU FATHER for the wonderful lectures of this day, Thank YOU FATHER for thy spirit of truth that abides with us, we thank YOU FATHER GOD for coming down on earth by THYSELF to fix things on earth and establish your administration on earth. Thank YOU FATHER GOD ALMIGHTY for making everything well. We have YOU Divine Spirit of Truth to guide and direct us. Thank you for correcting our spirit and for us to witness this wonderful Lecture Revelation. Thank YOU FATHER GOD*

Akwa Abasi Ibom **ETE** for directing us your children of Nditor Akwa Ibom, Thank **PAPA** for keeping us with you, we have **YOU FATHER GOD ALMIGHTY** and all is well with us, and **YOUR** entire creations.

Let thanks and praises be given to **THE FATHER** in the name of Our Lord Jesus Christ.

Let thanks and praises be given to **THE FATHER** in the blood of Our Lord Jesus Christ.

Let thanks and praises, power, dominion, majesty, supremacy, authority and adoration be ascribed to **THEE MOST HIGH GOD LEADER OLUMBA OLUMBA OBU, THE SOLE SPIRITUAL HEAD OF THE UNIVERSE, KIET-A-KIET ABASI** even, now and forever more. Amen!

Prayer by HRM Queen Disem Solomon David **ETE** to thank **THE FATHER GOD:**

Let thanks and praises be given to **THE FATHER GOD** in the name of Our Lord Jesus Christ.

Let thanks and praises be given to **THE FATHER GOD** in the blood of Our Lord Jesus Christ.

Let thanks and praises be given **THE FATHER GOD**, now and forever more. Amen!

We thank YOU FATHER GOD for this wonderful week of the Ark of the New Covenant of Love that YOU have established for us. We thank YOU for The Supreme Unity of Entire Nigeria and Africa Land. Thank YOU FATHER for coming to reveal the truth for us because YOU are THE HOLY SPIRIT OF TRUTH through which you give the ability for all your children to be able to live by truth.

Thank YOU FATHER OLUMBA OLUMBA OBU for this Lecture on Akwa Ibom State. Thank YOU FATHER for YOU has given us the understanding that Akwa Ibom is land of positive children of GOD. We thank YOU FATHER OLUMBA OLUMBA OBU that you have come to unite the whole world with the understanding that Africa is the mother and fatherland. Thank **YOU FATHER** for making so that all thy children to dwell in peace because Peace means the opening gate for everything and all is well with all your creation, now and forever more.

Let thanks and praises be given to **THE FATHER GOD** *in the name of Our Lord Jesus Christ.*

Let thanks and praises be given to **THE FATHER GOD** *in the blood of Our Lord Jesus Christ.*

Let thanks and praises be given to **THE SUPREME BEING, THE AKWA, THE IBOM, THE ABASI, THE ALL AND ALL, THE TOTALITY OF EVERYTHING, THE SUPREME PEACE, THE SUPREME TRUTH, THE HOLY SPIRIT OF TRUTH** *who have come to establish truth in the whole world and all is well with YOUR entire creation, now and forever more. Amen!*

THANK YOU FATHER

Ndito Akwa Ibom and A True Nigerian Man & Woman

CHAPTER TWO

A TRUE NIGERIAN MAN AND WOMAN

FATHER'S TALK
(GOD PRESENT)

Friday Twenty-First Judas Iscariot FATHER Two Thousand and Eight (BI.OC.BOOH)
(21.03.2008)

In the name of Our Lord Jesus Christ, In the Blood of Our Lord Jesus Christ, Now and forever more

A TRUE NIGERIAN MAN AND WOMAN

Today! It pleases **ME THE FATHER GOD THE CREATOR OF THE UNIVERSE** to give this Lecture Revelation titled, **A TRUE NIGERIAN MAN AND WOMAN,** which is an additional Lecture Revelation to *THE NIGERIA IN THE AFRICA.*

INTRODUCTION

As I said, it is only The Holy Spirit that can give mankind ability to understand the WORD from **THE FATHER GOD** in **THE FATHER'S TALK (GOD PRESENT)**. It is not a made up WORD. It is not the WORD that came out after research. It is NOT a publication from any form of research. It is **FATHER'S TALK (GOD PRESENT)** WORD as The **WORD** talking for **HIMSELF.** Also, these WORDS do not come out from the studio of an ordinary soul. They are WORDS from **THE SUPREME WORD OF THE UNIVERSE HIMSELF, THE STUDIO OF ALMIGHTY FATHER GOD, THE UNIVERSAL SUPREME WORD WHICH IS THE SOUL OF MYSELF.** Therefore, **I THE FATHER GOD** through **MY DIVINE LOVE** requests that you, all mankind should have humility and ACCEPT The **TRUTH.**

The TRUTH is not because you like it. The TRUTH is the record that has been there right from the time of old which is now coming out for enlightenment.

I AM going to reveal something about **A NIGERIAN MAN AND WOMAN** that is,

THE TRUE NIGERIAN MAN AND A WOMAN, not the fake ones, not the corrupted ones, not ones from evil transits of birth into Africa. I mean a TRUE citizen who is an **AFRICAN.** I use **NIGERIA** as the focal point because of the Divine River Niger, but when I say **NIGERIA,** I mean **AFRICA,** the CENTRE of the whole world as, the First Port Of Call.

I want to defend The TRUTH NATURE of **A NIGERIAN MAN AND WOMAN.** Anybody that makes a trip to Africa that is, to any place in any of the African countries say, **NIGERIA** and meets a TRUE AFRICAN, meaning **A TRUE NIGERIAN MAN** OR **WOMAN** would come to know that they are very good and positive in nature.

They are very friendly, especially if you are a stranger. That was how Abraham and Sarah were because the blood of fatherhood and motherhood was in them.

A: **A GOOD CITIZEN OF NIGERIA**

Any GOOD citizen of **NIGERIA** is so easy to be entreated. There is no artificiality in such a person. He or she cannot be seen or termed as pompous. You can confirm this when you go to places such as **Calabar** areas, which are the **Efik** and **Ibibio** indigenes of **NIGERIA,** where the original children of **"EDIBU" EDISANA (HEBREWS)** are. Go and check for yourself. Also if you go to the **Hausas** and **Yoruba,** areas and some other places in **NIGERIA I** can mention, you will find that they are very humble. There are so many places and people like that all over **NIGERIA** and indeed the whole of **AFRICA.**

A **Calabar** man or woman of **NIGERIA,** who are the **Efik** and **Ibibio** people, especially the real **Calabar** person (THE EFIK), can leave their whole house for you to stay. They are very peaceful. Their duty is to sing songs and maintain things. They are called the **Maintainers,** the **Caretakers Of The Land. Efik** and **Ibibio** area of **NIGERIA** particularly is where you will see the TRUE fatherhood nature. **A TRUE NIGERIAN Efik** and **Ibibio** persons possess the TRUE fatherhood and motherhood Nature.

Different places in the world have different characters. There are some places in the world that have the character of a son. Other places have the character of a daughter and other characters of a mother or a father. All the characters of human beings are displayed at particular areas and places all over the world.

For instance, I gave **Britain** the character Of **Accommodation Spirit called 'AMIDIAN', THE COMBINED ENERGY** from **KING James.** I gave **America** Character Of **Improvement Spirit called 'U--VEFOROBEDIAN,** which is the ability to improve things that is, to help and make things work. I created all the places in this world with all the characters in them because it is only ONE PERSON that is ONE **SPIRIT SOUL** that established all the places of the world.

For the whole of **AFRICA** especially **NIGERIANS** and particularly the **Efik** and **Ibibio** people of the south-eastern part of the country, I gave them the characters of the father and the mother, the **Caretaker Character**. They can accommodate people and are very, very peaceful. They are very, very peaceful when it comes to what peacefulness is because it is only the father and mother that takes care and tolerates their children. Therefore, **A TRUE NIGERIAN** as a whole can NEVER be a DUPER. **A TRUE NIGERIAN NEVER DUPES**.

A TRUE NIGERIAN can NEVER be someone that people have the impression that they are very bad and corrupt. Watch and see that type of a **NIGERIAN** person. You will come to see and conclude that such a person is a FAKE **NIGERIAN,** not the person that misbehaves because of a very severe bad condition.

Like some people parade the words from pillar to post that **NIGERIANS** are very corrupt set of people. You have never met **A TRUE AND GOOD NIGERIAN** if you have that impression or have had a bad experience with an imposter.

Who you meet mostly depends on what you did therefore, what were you doing and how did you manage to meet such a person? Where did you go? Who connected you? Who did you meet and what sort of dealings transpired between you? Was it a government personnel or individual good or bad citizens that you met and had business with? As the saying goes birds of the same feather fly together.

 I, THE FATHER GOD ALMIGHTY is correcting these bad impressions about **THE NIGERIAN PEOPLE** and **NIGERIA** where **THE DIVINE RIVER NIGER, MY SUPREME SPIRIT "AIR" WAS ON TOP OF THE RIVER NIGER "WATER" BEFORE THE GEN OF THE SPOKEN WORD WAS FORMED** through this Lecture Revelation. The place called "UWANAIBOM" OR URUAN, but is now Akwa Ibom State called URUAN **"UWANA INYANG"** meaning **RIVER LIGHT** which was the place I brought out light to cover the whole earth and make a day before even the creation of mankind. **I THE FATHER GOD ALMIGHTY AM THE SUPREME AIR AND WATER THAT FORMED THE DAY AND NIGHT IN AFRICA.**

 The **NIGER DELTA** of **NIGERIA** IS THE PLACE THAT I BROUGHT OUT **LIGHT** TO COVER THE WHOLE EARTH. (**UTINIDEM ABASI**). Therefore, if today some evil spirit-souls have gone and manifested physically there to cause havoc and mar the true image of the country and the good citizens, do not generalize those evil characters to the **TRUE NIGERIAN MEN AND WOMEN.**

Before now all evil people starting from the president, governors and many others occupying prominent positions, including some preachers and many evil people that struggled for power killed people and caused all sorts of problems in the whole of **AFRICA,** especially in the country of **NIGERIA.** They are the foreign spirits that trouped to manifest there physically as human beings because of what **I THE FATHER GOD** has put in place in the Continent of Africa. Nevertheless, the **SECURITY I** put in place will NEVER allow those operations of evils to work there anymore from now upward!

Let **ME** INFORM the whole universe and all **NIGERIANS,** that **I THE FATHER GOD ALMIGHTY THE CREATOR OF THE UNIVERSE, THE UNIVERSAL SUPREME WORD** have MARKED OUT **NIGERIA AS THE SEAT OF MY POSITIVE SUPREME OPERATIONS FOREVER WHETHER ANYONE LIKE IT OR NOT**.

If **NIGERIA** and the whole of Africa is not THE SEAT OF **MY SPIRITUAL OPERATIONS** where I earmarked for **MY DIVINE** purposes before the foundation of world, **NIGERIA** would have been a forgotten place because so many nations envy **NIGERIA AND THE WHOLE AFRICA.** So many people in this world want to get rid of that glory and take the place. Nonetheless, **I AM** telling you that ONE WITH GOD IS THE MAJORITY. In terms of wisdom, in terms of peace, in terms of anything good and I mean anything good and positive, you should go to **NIGERIA** and you will find it there.

Now! I have changed the bad contents of the **NIGERIANS** and I REBUKE all those bad spirits-souls that 'they' sent to come and spoil the country when they wanted to make **NIGERIA** a dumping ground just as it happened in Babylon. However, today! I have saved **NIGERIA** from that dumping situation.

NIGERIA WILL BE THE LEADER.

NIGERIA IS A TEACHER OF ALL THE NATIONS.

A TRUE NIGERIAN, meaning a GOOD CITIZEN OF **NIGERIA,** is very PEACEFUL. He or she is a PEACEMAKER. **A TRUE NIGERIAN** is very knowledgeable and has humility. They like strangers as well as good things.

The foreign people born there are the ones causing all the problems in **NIGERIA** and for **NIGERIA.** These foreign people born in **NIGERIA** are the ones that practice witchcraft. They kill people and formulate all sorts of evil activities because they are directed by witchcraft, as they are agents of witchcraft. They do rituals and look for money through all sorts of evil means. They siphon money in a bid to deplete the wealth of the nation and cause the downfall of the country because wherever there is LIGHT, Satan as darkness, would go there to quench the light. Nonetheless, it will NEVER work.

Changes for good have been going on in **NIGERIA** since the year two thousand and one to date. The whole world will see what **NIGERIA** will become in the very near future and indeed what the whole of **AFRICA** will become because **I, THE**

FATHER GOD have conquered all the evil there, and I have put the peaceful leaders in place to lead the nation from now onwards, many positive soul of natural fathers has been manifested in Africa and western world, the same copy of that spirit soul is Nelson Mandela, Barack Obama President of USA, Umaru Musa Yar' Adua, the current President of Nigeria, Godswill Akpabio Governor of Akwa Ibom State of Nigeria, Clinton of USA, Donald Duke of Calabar Nigeria and Justus O. Mugbeh of BCS Nigeria, many of them in Africa and in the whole world which are not mention here now.

I gave *"Strengthen"* same spirit-star to a lot of people not mentions here that are positive.

I gave that *Strengthen* spirit-soul to so many people but they swapped over to negativism.

B: A GOOD CITIZEN OF AFRICA

AFRICANS as a whole are very accommodating. An **AFRICA** man will leave his house for you to sleep in and would sleep outside if need be. When you see a good citizen of **AFRICA,** you would come to know that they are very hospitable.

An **AFRICAN** man is a father just as **I AM THE FATHER** because **AFRICA** IS THE FATHER OF ALL NATIONS. Consequently, a typical and correct **AFRICAN** is somebody that can withstand a lot of things. What the 'Blackman', the **AFRICANS,** the **solid-skin** humans can withstand others cannot. However, as a matter of fact there is nothing like **black** and there is nothing like **white** as far as the colour of the human beings are concerned. The human beings you term **black** to be the colour of their skin is not correct. They should be appropriately and correctly referred to, as **thick-skin** or **solid-skin** or **dark-skin** human beings. There is no man or woman of **AFRICA** and of **AFRICAN** descent that is black. **I AM** correcting that impression and expression now. There is NOTHING like a Blackman or Whiteman or a coloured person. THERE IS NO COLOUR THAT CAN BE ATTRIBUTED TO A HUMAN BEING. The only thing you should attribute to any human being in terms of colour of skin is, **dark-skin** or

solid-skin or **thick-skin** and **light-skin** or **soft-skin**. A 'Whiteman' has **light skin** or **soft skin** or **fair skin**.

The group of humans you refer to, as Blackman is **dark-skin** or **solid-skin** or **thick-skin** persons. These groups of people have **thick** and **solid** skin and are **dark** in complexion but NOT **black**. They are **SOLID** human beings in all aspects of things and from every indication. **AFRICANS** are **SOLID** human beings.
 If you check the origin of any human being that is solid, you will find that he or she is connected to **AFRICA**. They have spread all over the world. And their genes are very strong. When the genes of a **solid-skin** person entered any other human's body, it takes supreme because that is the original human being. **AFRICANS** have **thickness** of skin and are **solid** both in the blood and in the heart. An African can withstand anything and any condition. Therefore, an **AFRICAN** person should not be pompous. The original **AFRICAN** persons have humility because they are the fathers and the mothers.

The reason **I AM** giving this Lecture Revelation is that I want all **AFRICANS** to know that they are the **Caretakers** of the whole world and that they have the characters of a father and mother and also that he who laughs last will laugh the best.

The reason **AFRICANS** tend to be poor is because of their sin in the Garden of Eden because where you commit sin Satan destroys that place.

Today however, I HAVE RESTORED THE GLORY OF **AFRICA.** Nobody will succeed to use cunning to achieve anything from any **AFRICAN** person. Nobody can dupe any **AFRICAN** again. Really in truth, I have now mixed-up everybody. Some **light-skin** (Whiteman) humans are **AFRICAN** in nature and some of the **dark-skin AFRICANS** are **light-skin** European or Americans in nature. I have mixed everyone soul for good. As a result, now the whole world is one. ONE WORLD!

TO MAKE THE WHOLE WORLD ONE IS A TASK THAT MUST BE DONE.

Now! As the whole WORLD is ONE, I don't want to hear any **AFRICAN** say, "this is what 'Whiteman did to me." Also I don't want to hear any European or American say, "This is what **Blackman** did to me." Nobody did anybody anything! **I, THE FATHER GOD** has forgiven everyone and I have brought everybody together to be one.

What I will not tolerate however, is wickedness, hatred and suppression of others. If you are a good father or a good mother, take care of your children. Make sure that where you live is good. Condition it to be so.

This is the sign of being good. THE WHOLE WORLD SHOULD REVERSE THEIR ATTITUDE AND INCLINATIONS AND RETRACE THEIR STEPS TO **AFRICA.** They should go back to building all the nations of **AFRICA** because where your father is, that is your place. It may be called a village or old Home but when you have visitors or get married, or do any other important celebrations, you take your friends to your father's compound and not your own home no matter how beautiful your place is. We call it *ESIT EKWERRE* or *EKWERRE ETE.*

EKWERRE ETE means the family compound square. This is where the family and all the extended family can all gather together and discuss important things including important family matters.

In that light, the important things of this world are manipulated and engineered and controlled as well as refurbished in **AFRICA** because that is the **source** and **destination.** Subsequently, the whole wide world with **love** and **peace** should put their hands together and rebuild the whole of **AFRICA** because that is your father's home. **AFRICA** IS YOUR FATHER'S HOME. A good son and a good daughter should build a good house for their father. This is what the whole world MUST do.

America and Britain in particular should reverse their actions and focus a good level of attention on **AFRICA** if they want things to continue to be good for them.

THIS IS THE **VOICE** OF **THE FATHER GOD** TALKING. It is up to you to believe whether it is a man talking or **THE FATHER GOD ALMIGHTY** that is talking. Nonetheless, THE TRUTH STANDS FOREVER.

A good **AFRICAN** person should not be involved in witchcraft, should not join any secret society and should not indulge in using talisman or practicing any fetishism.

Egypt was to be **MY** physical place of glory but when Satan went and established the port of evil in Egypt, I took the glory away from there. When King Solomon went to promote the god of Sheba as the god of sexuality, I reacted accordingly.

You should know this; the god of Sheba was not actually evil, she was the spirit that controlled wealth and lived in the water called **mermaids** but they produce energy through sexuality and that became evil because that is what they brought to use to destroy Solomon. However, the woman they sent to carry out that assignment could not destroy King Solomon rather I captured her and made her to become the daughter of God and till today she is the daughter of God. That meant that the kingdom of this world has become the kingdom of **GOD** and **HIS** Christ. That was what took place through King Solomon.

Things worked out as they did because:
Solomon stands for **plentiful**.
Queen Sheba stands for **wealth**.
And **Bathsheba** the mother of Solomon means **abundance**. That also, is the

meaning of Sarah. Sarah also means Queen or Princess and all of them were original copies of Eve and Adam.

C: A GOOD CITIZEN OF THE WORLD

A good citizen of the whole world must practice LOVE ONE ANOTHER. A good citizen of the world must love everybody and must not look at the skin colour or which part of the world the other person is from.

This Lecture Revelation is to bring everybody together.

A TRUE NIGERIAN MAN AND A TRUE NIGERIAN WOMAN can be seen in the United Kingdom and in America and all the places of the rest of world and would be **true man** and a **true woman**. Also a good citizen of Britain is a good citizen everywhere in the world. All the people that are good in any country of the world are good in all the countries of the world.

When someone says 'I am born again' for instance it is likely that the church your parents worship is no longer good for you so have joined another. However, you forget that wherever you go you are what you are. So, if for instance, you were a prostitute in a church and then you go to a born-again church you still remain a prostitute if you continue to practice such, unless of course Christ changes you.

It is not the name that changes anyone. It is the spirit that you take evolution to that will change you. Hence, the truth remains the truth and unchangeable therefore what you cannot do is to play dumb with this knowledge. You must understand that if you move with arm robbers you must surely be an armed robber and remain so. If you move with prostitutes you are a prostitute. Also, if you move with someone who is in darkness, then you are in darkness therefore it is only when you move away from a bad spot that your life can change.

D: GOOD SONS AND DAUGHTERS OF THE FATHER GOD

A good citizen of **NIGERIA**, a good citizen of **AFRICA** and a good citizen of the world is going to be a good daughter or good son of **THE FATHER GOD**. What then is the difference in all places? Wherever you are and you are good there, you are good for **THE FATHER GOD** but if you are bad, you are Satan's offspring. That is what it is.

This Lecture Revelation is to support **THE NIGERIA IN AFRICA** to clearly give enlightenment so that people will not misinterpret the Divine Will of **THE FATHER GOD**.

E: LIKE A POSITIVE CALABAR (EFIK AND IBIBIO) PERSON

When you meet a positive **Calabar (Efik and Ibibio)** man or woman, they are very nice and are homely. The type of character the **Efik** and **Ibibio** men and **Efik** and **Ibibio** women possess cannot be seen in any place in the whole world, when it comes to carefulness and fatherhood and motherhood. And that is the truth.

Go and check it for yourself and you will see the type of peace that is in them. This is because they are the real children of **THE FATHER GOD**. However, they are not being treated well. As a result, a **Calabar** person looks like a coward if you come across them somewhere.

If you keep an **Efik** or **Ibibio** person with you, expect honesty because they are very honest set of people. Such persons will not eat your money and will not eat your food. **I AM** talking about true full-blooded **Calabar (Efik** and **Ibibio)** person, not the mixtures. He or she will never misplace your things and will never insult you.

A true **Efik** and **Ibibio** woman will take care of you very well regardless of anything because they are servants of **GOD** and they are caretakers. They are the mothers and the fathers. That is what everybody should know.

I spread the true **Calabar (Efik and Ibibio)** man and woman everywhere to establish this type of life. For instance, there is a part of Ghana that the people from there are typical **Calabar (Efik and Ibibio)** persons. And you will not see arrogance in that area. You will see a peaceful life. You will see them to be very, very close to their fathers and mothers. Zimbabwe also has typical **Calabar (Efik and Ibibio)** people in certain parts of the country.

There are typical **Calabar** people in all parts of **AFRICA,** the original Hebrew. You will see them in various places in **AFRICA** and they are always very peaceful and would run away from trouble.

Whenever they are somewhere and trouble erupts, they will pack up leave the place. That is why they are scattered everywhere. They are usually very dark in complexion and thick in the body. Most of them have thickness of the skin and are dark in complexion. If you come across a very typically dark, strong and solid person whether European, American or **AFRICAN** anywhere in the world, such a person has **Calabar (Efik** and **Ibibio)** origin in him or her.

Calabar was where **THE FATHER GOD** landed after the universal flood at the time of Noah. I will now tell you what actually happened when **THE FATHER GOD** landed there.

When that great universal flood happened during the time of Noah, it took Noah's Ark far, far away and then went past the land sea of India and came to China and I stopped there.

There is a place in China that is an everlasting dry land. I started the rainbow where that dry land in China is, because I did not let the flood destroy that place for a reason. That is original place where I preserved the seeds of fruits, leaves and all sorts of plants and things during that universal flood. That place is called **Lanshinshang,** unless of course the Chinese have changed the original name of that place to something else. Nevertheless, the original name of that place is **Lanshinshang** and it is China's landmark.

Being that I preserved fruits and herbs there naturally, I did not let the flood destroy that place. So, when the floodwater had to go, the water had to return to **Odu idem Abasi. MYSELF** is **ODU IDEM ABASI** where the water came out from to flood the whole world. The water came from up and from the ground.

Consequently, after it had performed its duty I had to send the waters back from where it came. That action of receding waters dragged the Ark of Noah backwards. And where did it land? It landed at "OKWOK ODRUK" (OKWOK ORUK) **Esuk**

Orok in **Calabar** originally is where the waster started to come and go before the water naturally dried and that was where the Ark of Noah came and landed. There is a part of Noah's Ark (some wood of the Ark) still in that sea till today.

Do you see the Cameroun Mountain; I pumped up the ground in that spot during the flood and that is the mountain. It was on top of that mountain that I spoke out to the waters and the waters went away and then grounded the Ark and then dragged it and eventually the Ark of Noah stopped at ***Esuk Orok.*** That is the reason I say to you that the **source** is the **destination. AFRICA** is the original place made by **THE FATHER GOD** and not by man.

F: I THE FATHER GOD THE CREATOR OF THE UNIVERSE SPREAD MY POSITIVE SELVES TO MANIFEST IN AFRICA

I spread **MY POSITIVE SELVES** to manifest in **AFRICA. MY** positive selves are the heart of love, the heart of peace and the heart of humility. It is natural system as something that is not changeable no matter what.

The light-skin human beings have tried every possible means to change the dark-skin human beings to be like them but it has not been possible.

The dark-skin person would shrug off whatever he or she has supposedly learnt from their light-skin counterpart and go right back to how he was. Such attitude of the dark-skin human being does not spell stupidity. It does not mean they do not want to learn or can't understand. That attitude is just the nature of the dark-skin human beings. They are natural people. Having clarified that, now **I AM** going to make **AFRICANS** to be more natural as well as more spiritual. From natural you get spiritual.

When Adam was natural in the Garden of Eden He was in **AFRICA.** Now, as Adam has become spiritual, HE is also in **AFRICA.** That is why **AFRICA** is **natural** and **spiritual.**

The other set of humans are artificial human beings. These are the people that believe too much in artificial things and carnal things. They are photocopied human beings. They are human beings that are products of photocopying. They are the manipulated human beings and as a result, they also like to manipulate things. They are themselves manipulators. They do not allow things to be natural. All the people that like to manipulate things are the ones fighting against **THE FATHER GOD.**

Who manipulates your things? It is somebody who is jealous of you and somebody that wants to discredit you. A talented person manufactures something direct from himself or herself. A talented person is not somebody who copies things.

I don't want to go deep into this matter. This Lecture Revelation is a true witness to let you know yourself, so that you would not try to change your nature.

A TRUTHFUL AFRICAN and **A TRUTHFUL CITIZEN OF THE WORLD** should like to be natural and more spiritual. Allow things to be the way **THE FATHER GOD** wants them to be.

You can improve yourself with love, with mercy, with oneness and with righteousness. Extend human rights to everyone because they are selves that have the right to exist.

You should not change the natural look of things. If you do, you are fighting against **Nature** and **THE FATHER GOD** then the consequences await you. The group of human beings who fight against Nature should know that the consequences that await them in the very near future is very great. It is going to be dire for them.

G: A GREAT CHANGE IN THE LIVES OF INDIVIDUAL HUMAN BEINGS IN NIGERIA, AFRICA AND ALL NATIONS

From now on be very observant. After the year Two Thousand and One, I started to manifest so many people. Many spiritually mature people are born as elevated spirits that I have transferred from America, Jerusalem, Israel, the United Kingdom and China and all over the world. I transferred them from these places and sent them to manifest in **AFRICA** to help **AFRICA,** to assist their **FATHER'S** land to improve.

Do not say or even think that simply because you are dark-skin African now that you are not a light-skinned European or American. Do you know where you were born before? Do you know where you were previously that I transferred you? Just like HRM King Solomon David Jesse **ETE** whom I transferred from Israel to United Kingdom and from the United Kingdom now to **AFRICA** at **Ikot-Okwo, Akwa Ibom State, Nigeria.** Why did I do that? It is because I want Him to go and help the environment there, to help sort out the original place.

The place that you must go last is where you first came from. When you finish your transits, you go back to where you first manifested on earth. That is how The Nature works and that is what The Nature arranged.

Now, every human being should love one another. They should believe that they are from one father and one mother. They should believe in Brotherhood, which is the same parents, the same family of **THE FATHER GOD.**

CONCLUSION A: I THE FATHER GOD PROMISED THAT ETHIOPIA SHALL RISE

When I promised that 'ETHIOPIA SHALL RISE' this is the fulfilment of that promise, It is to send the good **SELVES** of **THE FATHER GOD;** the good positive WORDS back to **AFRICA** and back to the world. All the WORDS of **THE EVERLASTING GOSPEL** and all WORDS of **THE FATHER'S TALK (GOD PRESENT)** will manifest as human beings.

I have made A NEW **COVENANT OF LOVE** that HRM King Solomon David Jesse **ETE** who is incarnate soul of Abel as the budded improved product of **THE FATHER GOD** through whom I will engineer seventy-two million copies of Senior Servants of **THE FATHER GOD** on earth. These Servants are with different mansions as different talents that will be the Servants of **THE FATHER GOD.** They will be the Children of **THE FATHER GOD** that will serve **THE FATHER GOD.** They will constitute the original spreading offspring of Abel for eternity. If therefore, you behave well, I will use your house and put one of those spirits souls to come back on earth and serve **THE FATHER GOD.** If you do not behave well, then I will put you in the wastebasket because I have already made the provision for Seventy-two million Servants of **THE FATHER GOD** to be born on earth, in the spirit of Solomon who is peace.

These Servants of **THE FATHER GOD** are the peacemakers. They shall be called Children of **GOD.** They are as many as seventy-two million. So, if you are not a peacemaker, I will not use your house of your soul.

CONCLUSION B: **SATAN HAS NO SEAT OR TEMPLE IN NIGERIA OR IN ANY OF THE AFRICAN NATIONS NOT ANYWHERE IN THE ENTIRE WORLD.**

Satan has no seat in **NIGERIA.** He has no portion. He has no place to live. Hence, whatsoever evil you see happening now in the world is a temporary evil. As time goes on I will eradicate all evils in all parts of the world, especially in **NIGERIA** and the whole of **AFRICA.**

All evil will be eradicated in the whole world. People's minds will be corrected. Everybody will love one another. They will be good governments all over the countries of the world.

The whole world has been struggling all these years to make Nigeria good so that they can invest properly there. Now, **THE FATHER GOD** has answered your prayers.

THE FATHER GOD has answered the prayers of United Kingdom for **NIGERIA** to be good. **THE FATHER GOD** has answered the prayers of America for **NIGERIA** to be good. **THE FATHER GOD** has answered the prayers of the whole world that **NIGERIA** should be good, that **AFRICAN** countries should be good so that they can all go back there and to relax and manage things.

You should not go there for taxing and managing purposes. Rather go back there and develop the place but do NOT destroy any natural thing. YOU MUST NOT DESTROY ANY NATURAL THING IN DEVELOPING **AFRICA**. If you go there to destroy any natural thing you will be in trouble – big trouble!

Go there with courtesy. Go there and pay homage to your father's land, where in turn you will be blessed with honey and milk. That is what it is.

Wherever you go in **AFRICA** you will be blessed with **honey** and **milk** because it is your father's land. And your mind should be to go there to help, just like you would visit your father to pay homage to him. You would not go empty handed to go to see him. Likewise here, go to **AFRICA** with all the knowledge, all the wealth and everything you know to be positive. Don't go there with anything that is negative. If you disobey this, **I THE FATHER GOD** will thwart you! And **I** will deal with you!

Do not be surprised when you cannot succeed there in any program that is not good. The hand of **GOD THE FATHER, THE FATHER GOD** is in **AFRICA**. I HAVE ALREADY ESTABLISHED **MY** SEAT IN ALL THE LANDS IN ALL OF **AFRICA,** IN THE NAME AND BLOOD OF OUR LORD JESUS CHRIST. Amen

CONCLUSION C: IN THE SPIRIT THERE IS A SPIRITUAL AND PHYSICAL SWORD AS THE WORD OF GOD TO CUT DOWN ANY TREE THAT DOES NOT BEAR GOOD FRUITS IN NIGERIA, AFRICA AND THE ENTIRE WORLD.

In spirit, spiritual sword and physical sword have been blessed and sealed **OBEGO!** That everything must be positive in the world and in Africa and in Nigeria.

If any spirit or soul or human being goes there to plant anything that is not good that sword will cut it down. No bad fruit should be planted or put there. That time has passed.

Therefore, if you go to **AFRICA** to do business or if you go to any place in the world to do any business, be sure that what you have in mind is positive and also that your plan is positive. If it is negative you will see what will happen to you. That is **MY WORD**.

THIS WORD IS NOT FROM HUMAN BEING. THIS WORD IS FROM **THE FATHER GOD ALMIGHTY.**

NOW, LET MY PEACE AND BLESSING ABIDE WITH THE ENTIRE WORLD, NOW AND FOREVER MORE. AMEN!

THANK YOU FATHER!

Ndito Akwa Ibom and A True Nigerian Man & Woman

PART THREE

THE FORERUNNER
(I AM BEFORE AND BEHIND YOU)

FATHER'S TALK
(GOD PRESENT)

Date: OC/OF/OF (The third of June two Thousand and Six)

In the Name of Lord Jesus Christ
In the Blood of Lord Jesus Christ
Now and forever more

THE FORERUNNER
(I AM BEFORE AND BEHIND YOU)

Yes, I promised that today, I will come to reveal one of the most important things called the **FORERUNNER** in the context of **THE FATHER GOD**. Today is what? It is OC/OF/OF answered *Queen Disem*. That is right, the **FORERUNNER (I AM** before and behind you). **I THE FATHER GOD THE CREATOR OF THE UNIVERSE, THE A-Z**, brings this Revelation Lecture today to mark out the beginning of this third month of the year. The **WISDOM** of **THE FATHER** is greater than all wisdom. For **THE**

FATHER to make things perfect in the forward future **FORWARD EVER** is the reason why in the beginning I bring the **FORERUNNER** to streamline things but when I send things as **FORERUNNERS**, to streamline things, the lower people do not understand. Every aspect of life has a **FORERUNNER** and that is the point that I want to make. Every phase of life has a **FORERUNNER** because without a **FORERUNNER** what you do will not be meaningful.

Some people believe that **THE FATHER GOD THE CREATOR OF THE UNIVERSE** did not know what will happen in the Garden of Eden. They blame **ME THE FATHER GOD** by saying things such as, 'why should this happen and that happen, why should Adam eat that fruit in the garden of Eden and why should that become a problem and blah, blah, blah'. That is how man understands things. When I, **THE FATHER GOD** said that I regretted creating man, I did not actually regret creating man as such. It was a slip of tongue. Why should I, **THE FATHER GOD** regret creating man when I know that man represents **ME, THE FATHER GOD** and I **LOVE** man therefore man represents **LOVE**, and that makes man **THE FORERUNNER** of **MY GLORIOUS EVERLASTING**. Adam in particular as the King of Kings and the Lord of Lords is The Father of all creation in the physical realm, and in Adam is **MY SPIRIT OF ALL THINGS** as **THE FATHER** of all creation **THE MAKER, THE SPOKEN WORD** and the Son of **GOD**. Adam was the physical house that the **WORD** built for **HIMSELF**. When you want to spread something and make it plural, there is a particular way you will behave to make a situation change and take a plural shape. To split things you must bring confusion, because when things are stuck too much together you cannot break them. Whether they are good or they are evil. If you want to separate evil from good, you have to bring confusion amongst the two of them because without that they cannot break away and the evil will continue to confuse the good. Therefore every single idea comes out from **ME THE FATHER GOD THE CREATOR OF THE UNIVERSE** and I make each of them the **FORERUNNER** to lead and pave the way for something whether you call it good or bad.

A **FORERUNNER** means to pave the way for something, to prepare the road. How would a road work well? First of all, when there was no road at all the land was the Atlantic Ocean to be crossed; some were streams, others were water, forest, hills etc. If you want to put a road in such a place, you will first have to send a surveyor to survey the place and to form the shape that the road will take. There will be special instruments and skilled people that will cut the track and use their instruments to survey how the road will be built. First of all, the designer will design the road and he will decide on the length of the road, the width of the road, where it would start, and where it would stop. Would it have branches, such as A1, A2, 'M' this and 'M' that, so on and so forth, when the designer designs all these things as the architect then the engineer will be brought in to measure the road from the beginning to the end and to look at all the details such as diversions, among others. It is only at this point that they will know the actual cost of the road and the type of materials that they will need to construct the road. And this is the work of the **FORERUNNER**.

Now that the cost of the road is known and the materials that are required are also known, you may decide to publicise the project, or chose a construction company that will handle the job for you. Before the construction company starts work, they will have to take their own Engineers, their **FORERUNNER** to inspect the project, view the sight and size of the job before they will know how much to charge and then they will tender a quote. Once this is done they will estimate the time it will take and how the money will be produced and paid and so on and so forth before the work actually starts. All the different areas pertaining to the work will also have their **FORERUNNERS** in different ways.

The idea for making the road can be for the purpose of connecting one city to another city. What will the connection be for? It can be that there is something in the city that the road is built towards or in the path of the road which will actually instigate the road construction. There has to be a reason why the road is been built. The road is not the reason itself but there must be a road before the purpose can be achieved. You may want to build an industry at the other end of the road and what will be produced at that industry would need to be carried out to the open market therefore the road would be needed. And even the building of the industry itself requires a road for movement to and fro from the sight. All these need **FORERUNNERS** before the actual project of the road construction starts. When it reaches this stage and the construction company has signed an agreement they will go and inspect the sight where they will be based to start the work and keep their materials for the job. This place needs to be a mini city, a home, a quarter, an office where they will have telephones, water, light, petrol station among others but this will not be permanent. After the construction they will take these things away or they may decide to keep that place for a permanent contact, but there must be a reason why they would remain there. After that the road will start and the first thing that will happen is that they will bring in bulldozer's and a caterpillar machine and people to bulldoze the road and make tracks where the road will run and these tracks will be four times the size of the actual road. They will clear the place; remove all trees and all hindrance from the road. They will make it rough, scatter, and bulldoze everything away then they will remove the bad sand and reveal the land. They will then press it hard and put bridges and build other things such as gutters and pavements. They will put a water main and everything else that would be needed for a solid road construction before they start to tar and to coat it. First coat, second coat, two layers, three layers, and a fourth layer before the road would be ready for general public use and the generality of travel. From this stage, they can now convey things to the main site or to the industrial site or use the road for the main purpose which is to link to another village or city or whatever reason for the construction of the road. All these actions show and prove that there must be a **FORERUNNER** before the main job. When the job is over, the inspector will go there and inspect the job before the final payment will be paid and so on and so forth.

Now, coming back to **MY** way of doing things, **I THE FATHER GOD,** created man in **MY** own image and likeness and this image and likeness is what I have given as an example above. The way that I do things in spirit is the same way that man does things physically. Before anything establishes in spirit, there must be a way, a plan and a project and program and that program would sometimes manifest physically but other times it may only be based in the spirit. During all these things it is only **ME THE FATHER GOD** and **MY** workers that know what is going on and how to handle it, therefore have patience and tolerate the situation because the **FORERUNNER** is at work. When the **FORERUNNER** does not finish his or her work, and give a report back to show that the way is clear through surveying the place the actual work can never start. Within all these systems and formula's it is **ME THE FATHER GOD, THE CREATOR OF THE UNIVERSE.** I can make **MYSELF** in many dual capacities, reasons, positions, and parts among other things but at the end of the day, if I put **MYSELF** back, I become a **WHOLE**.

Do you not know that before a tree bears fruit there is a flower and it will be after that flower that the fruit will come up. Before a girl reaches the age of pregnancy, she will first menstruate to show that anything can happen after that. Any girl that begins to menstruate can also become pregnant that is a **FORERUNNER**. This is the reality. The same thing happens whenever you see any problem. I will send a **FORERUNNER** there to inspect the place and most of the time when the work is going on, that is when there are problems. Therefore I want everybody to understand that **I THE FATHER GOD, I AM ALL** and **ALL! THE FATHER GOD** is the **ALL** knowing **FATHER** and nobody knows the way of **THE FATHER GOD** but **THE FATHER GOD** knows everyone and the best way forward.

Before I send any of **MY** children, I send a **FORERUNNER**. For instance John the Baptist was a **FORERUNNER** for Jesus the

Christ and he was His relation. You cannot be a **FORERUNNER** to an outsider that you do not know. It is the person that knows you that can promote you. Nobody can promote Brotherhood of the Cross and Star, or promote the **KING OF KINGS** without a **FORERUNNER,** who is His own relation or His own spirit soul in a different form. What was the relationship between John the Baptist and Jesus the Christ? Everybody knows the answer to that. If you know the relationship in both the spiritual and physical, then you will know why he was the **FORERUNNER**. Another person cannot scratch someone's itch (crow, crow) past the waist. If you go beyond the waist you are looking for trouble. It is only your own person that has the right to go beyond the waist down. Therefore if you say that you want to promote **ME** and reveal **ME**, the first test would be, whether you even know yourself? Do you not know that John the Baptist knew who Christ was, and this is because one is the soul and the other is the spirit. It is the soul that promotes the spirit, while in turn the spirit promotes the soul. It is your carbon copy that knows you and you know your copy. You, the original copy, and your carbon copy must be one. If you marry a man who is not a part of you, then confusion will start. I have given so many instances in revelations that state that your **FORERUNNER** must be a part of you in a different copy to be able to reveal you and support you and stand with you and also know you enough to speak about you.

In the whole wide world, how many people know **THE FATHER GOD**? They do not know. **I THE FATHER GOD** is something that human beings are always confused about. The scientist and the philosophers and the so called prudent of this world talk about **THE FATHER GOD** but they are confused, because if you do not know yourself first you cannot know **THE FATHER GOD**. Therefore **I AM** not interested in the first instance about who knows **ME THE FATHER GOD** and who does not know **ME THE FATHER GOD** but you must know yourself first. When you know yourself first, then you will automatically know where you come from and who actually be your true **SPIRITUAL FATHER** and your **CREATOR**. As I have said previously, to believe something is one thing, but to know something is another thing. For all the time that people say that **OLUMBA OLUMBA OBU** is this and that, they only believe, but they do not know who **OLUMBA OLUMBA OBU** is. Maybe **OLUMBA** made your sickness to be over and therefore you believe **HIM** as **GOD**. Maybe **OLUMBA** talks very well, preaching, one way, or the other, or maybe you are following your father or your daughter or your mother to be saying that **OLUMBA** is **FATHER**. **OLUMBA** is this, and that, but can you prove it or you are just *follow, follow(following blindly)* If they tell you that A+A+B+F= AO and you have no idea that A is one and, B is two and F is six, then how will you add them together to get ten? On the other hand, if you are told that one + one + six, you will know that the answer is eight. To have the answer is one mark but how you managed to get the answer is the greatest mark that you must gain because you may have stolen it from someone. There is too much *follow, follow* (following blindly) in this world. That is why **I** must have a **FORERUNNER,** who is **MY** agent, the defender of truth and the defender of faith. It is He who knows **ME** that comes from **ME** that I will speak to and dwell with and talk through. A special assigned person to reveal **ME**. Do you think that the twelve disciples would have known our Lord Jesus the Christ because they were his disciples or Mary would have known our Lord Jesus the Christ because he is her son? Do you think that Mary Magdalene would have believed in Jesus the Christ because she is from Israel? Let **ME** tell you how all these people managed. First before Mary became pregnant, I sent a **FORERUNNER**. Angel Gabriel was the **FORERUNNER** to Mary's pregnancy. I made sure that I informed Mary in time that she would be impregnated by The Holy Spirit. **I AM** The Holy Spirit, **MY** potency and **MY REAL SELF INFLUENCE** is The Holy Spirit. Just like there is the negative influence.

When I called the seven spirits of creation to create via the WORD, the WORD did not manifest physically as a human being, but I create **Adam** and live in him as **THE WORD** because it was the potency of that WORD that I used in making creation, therefore, I kept one unused of **MY** Spirit –soul's. When you read Revelation chapter E (five), you will see where it is spoken about the seven spirits of creation that I sent to each generation.

Revelation E: E -H five: *five to eight.*
5 and one of the elders saith unto me, Weep not; behold, the Lion that is of the tribe of Judah, the Root of David, hath overcome to open the book and the seven seals thereof.
6 And I saw in the midst of the throne and of the four living creatures, and in the midst of the elders, a Lamb standing, as though it had been slain, having seven horns, and seven eyes, which are the seven Spirits of God, sent forth into all the earth.
7 And he came, and he taketh [it] out of the right hand of him that sat on the throne.
8 And when he had taken the book, the four living creatures and the four and twenty elders fell down before the Lamb, having each one a harp, and golden bowls full of incense, which are the prayers of the saints.

Do you see that? That is the Seven Spirits souls of **GOD** sent to all the earth.

These Seven Spirits were the first Seven Spirits that I projected out of **MYSELF** before the physical creation and I used six and remained one. I created from the first day of creation to the sixth day of creation when I created man, then I rested. The seventh day Spirit is the spirit that I used to manifest **MYSELF** in the birth of OUR LORD JESUS CHRIST so that the potency, as THE WORD ITSELF should come to manifest to save man out of the predicament of lowness and emptiness. And this was the access channel that I THE PERSONIFIED HOLY SPIRIT OF TRUTH will use to personally to come and streamline things physically on earth. Therefore, I sent the angel Gabriel to come as a **FORERUNNER** to inform Mary that that potency, the **WORD** will come through her. And whoever gives birth to the **WORD** has been given birth to by the **WORD**, so that it comes to pass that as a woman came out of a man so a man must come out of a woman. Because the potency of creation which is the total energy of **MYSELF** that came to this world to die, to kill the physical flesh of the mother earth and then come back with **ME** in the spirit to become one with **ME**, had to undergo the act of squeezing through the channel of a woman. And it is because of this that the angel Gabriel had to reveal the birth of Christ to Mary. Mary asked him how it will happen and angel Gabriel responded that it will be by the power of Holy Spirit of God and the influence of the Creator will be in you and Mary had the inspiration to believe it. Therefore, when Christ was born, Mary became a teacher as the mother of Christ and therefore passed the inspiration onto Christ but supposing there was no information as the **FORERUNNER**, how will this have been possible. There is no time that I do something without first of all sending a message to inform of the pending event but if the message is not passed on well with understanding then I will not allow the event to happen because there will be problems and confusion. Also if you do not listen to **ME** and develop your self-consciousness, I will not use you for any important event. I ask therefore, how people can believe that they can direct or give instruction in this Kingdom or do anything for **ME THE FATHER GOD** when they have no consciousness of who they are. You do not know yourself and you do not know **ME THE FATHER GOD**. Tell **ME** what type of vision are you seeing? Is it the vision of soothsayers, elementary vision, and *'copy, copy'* vision (coping others). **I AM** going to cut the story short, but for a long time now before even the birth of Our Lord Jesus Christ I first send a messenger before every event and programs that I put in place. Without information, I cannot do anything because when the information has not been received there will be confusion and that is why **I AM** the information. I send information to go first to enlighten people about what is coming and because of that, **MY** events always come. The problem with mankind is that they do not want to learn a lesson and they do not want to humble themselves and allow **ME THE FATHER GOD** to operate through them and that is why they see all these problems in the world today.

Even before Mary Magdalene believed in Jesus Christ as one of the greatest Messiahs, it was through John the Baptist. Mary Magdalene was an Israelite that loved John the Baptist and used to listen to him preaching. Do you know what happened? It was when they arrested John the Baptist that he told Mary that she should go and listen to the son of man because he is the one that testified about him. It was John the Baptist that always spoke to Mary because he knew that Mary was from his stock and he could not help her, but the greatest teacher could help her, therefore it was John the Baptist that introduced Mary Magdalene to Christ. When Mary went to listen to Christ, she knew that HE was the only one that could forgive her sin. Mary was practising prostitution out of annoyance with the condition that **GOD** was not there to help her. It was not part of her original template. That is why I say that you should forgive and forget because someone can do something but it may not be their own plan. It is negative control that is trying to grab the person away from **GOD** to use that person in the other side, but when I look at their face and see the mark of salvation, I go and get the person back. That is the work of a messenger. When Mary heard Jesus the Christ preaching she knew who He was because John the Baptist introduced Christ to her. The Disciples of

Christ who came and joined Christ eventually were introduced by John the Baptist. He told them that He is not the Messiah but the **FORERUNNER** to prepare their hearts for Christ. I can tell you many instances of **FORERUNNERS** such as before the birth of Isaac there was a **FORERUNNER**, a message given that Sarah will have a child and his seed will germinate all over the world. There was also a message for Abraham that his children would cover the world. One set from Ishmael and another from Isaac therefore these two sets of children cover the whole world. Now what else can you know without a **FORERUNNER**. That is the meaning of **I AM** before and behind you because when I send the information I must be before and behind **MY** messenger, the agent as I cannot leave **MY** agent comfortless.

Now I do everything for **MYSELF**. If anybody has consciousness of **ME THE FATHER GOD**, it means that I have consciousness of that person even before they are born and I program that person so that nothing can flag its wings in their direction, in the name of our Lord Jesus the Christ, *Amien.* For all these reasons, you must be aware that prophecy is information from a **FORERUNNER** from **GOD** about a pending event that will occur in due course. All the higher consciousness brethren are **MY FORERUNNERS** because before anything happens in their life, I have already told them. So that you will be careful and know how what form things will take before you reach your destination. Therefore the meaning of **I AM** before and behind you means that no rightful personality would send a messenger on an errand and allow that messenger to be lost no matter what happens because from the day that you call someone and send a message it means that the person is working for you. You become responsible of for how he travels and his life because he is on an errand for you. All **MY** children who testify about **ME** and know **THE FATHER** and release information about **THE FATHER** are those I have sent without sending you cannot do this. And if I send you it means that **I AM** then I will be with you, I will control you , I will guide you and I will protect you. I will reveal more and more things to you and the more truthful you are the more awareness and reward that you will receive in the name of Our Lord Jesus the Christ.

    A **LOVE** practitioner, a **MERCY** practitioner, a **KINDNESS** practitioner, a **PEACE** practitioner, and **TRUTH** practitioner are all good stars and they are **MY FORERUNNERS**. Anywhere that you see any of these good stars emerge and are practiced, know that place belongs to **THE FATHER** and that is the message of a **FORERUNNER**. That is the idea of a **FORERUNNER** and the sign that **THE FATHER** has taken glory in that place but where you see strife, jealousy, envy, maliciousness and all sorts of negative things and they tell you that they are working for **PAPA**, know that you are working for you own papa not **ME, PAPA**. Because you cannot work for **THE FATHER GOD** and hate, someone and you cannot work for **THE FATHER GOD** and gossip and have strife and jealousy and destroy.

Be aware of someone's character because I do not send groups to work for **ME**, I send individuals. If I say reverend, or father or pastor and so forth, that is only one person that I have ordered. When I say Christ Servant, I mean one person, one part of **ME**. No matter how many Christ Servants that there may be, they form only one person. If I say children of God that is one forty-four, thousand that is only one person as one part of **ME**. You are not the **WHOLE** therefore, if you do not **LOVE**, it means that you do not have consciousness of yourself and who you belong to and who you represent and therefore you are not a **FORERUNNER**. Know yourself and stand with the truth and know that at every stage, I have a proper message about that stage and if the message does not come from the proper channel then it is causing confusion. In your family, I have sent a **FORERUNNER** there before you are born. There is a message that you will be a child of God and you will work for God. Wherever the situation that you find yourself there is a **FORERUNNER**. Even in the village. I have set all normal systems and complete workers that will follow you before you are born. That is why in **THE FATHER'S** system there is no confusion because everything is demarcated. It works automatically because it is prearranged. Now **MY** duty is to give a proper awareness and a higher consciousness to **MY** children to work for **ME** in the correct way in the name of Our Lord Jesus the Christ Amen. This is the end of part one of the **FORERUNNER**.

SECTION TWO:
PEACE IS THE HIGHERSELF OF WISDOM

The **FORERUNNER** of every situation is **PEACE** because **PEACE** is the higher self of **WISDOM**, the centre, the bank, the memory, the **BOOM** and **THE EVERLASTING UNLIMITED MEMORY**. This **MEMORY** is where I store everything about **ME**. It is **MY FORERUNNER, MY PERSONAL FORERUNNER**. Any place where you do not see **PEACE**, forget about that place. You can be there on your own accord but to say that you are there for **THE FATHER GOD** is not true because I have not authorized it and there is no guarantee.

You can marry a beautiful wife but if she is not **PEACEFUL** she can fight you and tear your cloth. She can even close your eye. You can marry a handsome man who is not **PEACEFUL**, and you are beautiful, he can break your leg one day and that will be the end of your beauty. You become a one legged woman. Do not be attracted to anything that has no **PEACE**. If there is a bank that is full of money but there is no **PEACE** there and you go and touch that money, fire will burn you, and then confusion and trouble will start. You may even be arrested and that means that, that is not you money.

The **FORERUNNER** of anything that belongs to you is **PEACE**. The **FORERUNNER** character of any child of **GOD** must be **PEACE**. That is why it is said that blessed are the **PEACEMAKERS** for they shall be called the sons of **GOD, THE FATHER'S** children. I revealed to HRM King Solomon **ETE** about the bridge that I will bring to work with the **KING OF KINGS** and the **LORD OF LORD** called **PEACEMAKERS**, Children of God. When you read the book titled '***HE IS THE***

FATHER', you will read about these things. However any member of COG who is not a **PEACEMAKER** is not a child of God. He or she is a child of Satan. It was written in the Sermon of the Mount that the original FATHER who is your FATHER and **MY** son said that blessed are the **PEACEMAKERS** for they shall be called the sons of God. Therefore what type of a child of God are you when you do not have **PEACE** and you are not a **PEACEMAKER**. **AM I A FATHER** of trouble, **AM I A FATHER** of corny (trick), and **AM I A FATHER** who assassinates people's characters. **AM I A FATHER** that says that **I AM** the one to cork and crow? Look at this whole wide world that I have created and you believe that **I AM THE CREATOR OF THE UNIVERSE** but when or where do you hear **MY** voice on the street or where do you see **ME** claiming anything.

People go about raising their shoulders as the president, the head of state, and saying 'I am a commander in chief'. Do you hear that I have one day gone to bully them? Do the people of this world know that someone owns this world? Does that not show how deep **PEACE** is? Does that not show you how calm **I AM**? Look at all the nonsense, all the evil practice, and all the rubbish that people engage in this world but when do you see **ME**? You can see the difference now from when the angels used to take charge for **ME** that now there is **PEACE** everywhere. If **I** have to behave like any of you in this world that say I am in charge, I am a Head of State, I am a President, I am a King, I am a Servant, I do this and I do that, I am in charge and I do this in the name of God and *blah, blah, blah.* Tell **ME** how this world will *enter* (fit) **ME** and you. Where is the space for **ME** and you or anybody on this earth? Look at small, small, small second hand spirits, elementary spirits called the particle of creation making noise everywhere. Just like small, small, small generators making noise everywhere. Do you hear electricity make noise? It is only generators that make noise everywhere. Even a ten volt generator will make so much noise that you cannot hear anything in the vicinity but it cannot even charge batteries but when you come across electric power, do you hear any noise? That is **THE FATHER GOD THE CREATOR OF THE UNIVERSE**.

If you are not behaving in a **PEACEFUL** manner, quietly intelligently and knowledgeable as a **PEACEFUL** intellect, then forget about it. And forget about saying that you are attached to **ME**. You're deceiving yourself. That is why **I** say that every child of God must read this message. The **FORERUNNER** of **THE FATHER** itself is **PEACE**. **I AM LOVE** but where there is no **PEACE**, **LOVE** cannot reign, and therefore the practice of **LOVE** is defeated. Therefore, **MY FORERUNNER** of **LOVE** is **PEACE** and that is why you see that **PEACE** and **LOVE** are always together. That is why **I** say that you must try all possible means to have the **FIVE STARS** before you can be **MY** messenger and before **I** can use you effectively.

Song:
MERCY and **LOVE, RIGHTEOUSNESS, KINDNESS** and **PEACE** signify Brotherhood.

The above song signifies the family of the **FIVE STARS**. Read the lecture revelation titled *'INDESTRUCTIBLE FIVE STARS'* to learn more. Today, I reveal **MY FORERUNNER**, **MY** privacy, **MY** pant and **MY** inner bedroom, **MY** conserved area. If you really want to test your blood in order to know who your father is go to **PEACE**. I have revealed blood testing through the revelation lecture *'Spiritual Parent'*. Test your blood and you will know who your spiritual parent is through this Lecture Revelation. The instrument for this test is to know who you an offspring off and who you belong to and ask whether it is **PEACE**. When you cannot make **PEACE** and you cannot **LOVE**, you cannot have **KINDNESS**, you cannot have **MERCY** and cannot **FORGIVE**, and have no **RIGHTEOUSNESS** then forget about it. You can be created by **THE FATHER GOD** but you do not come from **THE FATHER GOD**. **I AM** sorry but furniture is not a living child. In the city of a nation, there are many roads and there are many things. Some things that are fanciful and moulded make the place a city. In the house where you dwell, there is the furniture that makes the house looks like a home but your children belong to you. You can change all the furniture anytime that you want to. When another company makes better furniture, I can change it as you know, one can change their furniture every six months if one wants but can I change **MY** child? A permanent office in **ME** is **PEACE**, **MY** children. Sometimes even a wife can be changed. You can leave her to go if she does not want to stay. Supposing that you do not want to practice **PEACE** claiming that **PEACE** is too much then you leave **MY** children of **PEACE** and go but you cannot take **MY** children with you. Any child that the wife takes with her does belong to that man.

When the mother God said that your **PEACE** is too much, I cannot take this again, I am going to have my Queendom, because I cannot share with your Kingdom, any child that followed her is no longer in the Kingdom rather he or she is in the Queendom. That is why you see so many children in the Queendom.

Consciousness of **PEACE** is the sign of **MY FORERUNNER** and **I AM** before and behind him and her from the BRINGSLIONS of the BRINGSLIONS. **I AM** before and behind him and her from the beginning to the forward ever. Therefore **PEACE** is the sign of been a child of God. A **PEACEMAKER** is a child of God. Be **PEACEFUL** and you will see **ME**, twenty-four hours, because you become **MY** integrity, **MY** intelligence, and **MY** sure banker. Therefore I have blessed this Lecture Revelation. Any soul that accepts this Lecture Revelation and follows it and identifies his blood, his spirit, his soul, his energy and his indwelling capacity within this Lecture Revelation is automatically **THE FATHER GOD'S** child and is **MY FORERUNNER** and I will use you extensively. I will use you to manifest **MY** glory and wherever **I AM** you will be there in the name of our Lord Jesus the Christ.

How will I talk through someone who is not **PEACEFUL** so that when you cause trouble, you leave **ME** on the road? You know you can be walking with someone to go somewhere and any small difficulty, you will be sorry for yourself. Any sign of any trouble, they will not be quiet and walk away, rather they start to argue and fighting may start but if you walk as a **PEACEMAKER** and try to maintain **PEACE** then you will walk away. Children of **PEACE** are **THE FATHER GOD'S** original inner soul and they promote **LOVE**. That is why wherever **LOVE** must be promoted, it is only **PEACE** that can promote it because how can you go and do charity and help people then, on the day when you are praying for people and one stupid spirit says 'you stupid man why are standing here praying'? As a result, you leave that prayer and start to quarrel with the people and at this point, your prayer spoils. That is why with the exception of **PEACE**, you cannot see **THE FATHER GOD** and with the exception of having a **PEACEMAKER'S** spirit, you cannot be a child of God. **I AM** sorry but there is nothing that you can do about it. There is no miracle or magic or any other way that you can attach to **ME** without being a **PEACEMAKER**. Therefore, you can be virgin, but not necessarily be a **PEACEMAKER**. There are people who go and consult juju that are told that they should not go closer to women. Does that mean that when they finish with the juju they will not break their virginity? Even juju knows that it has to penetrate your body and that can only work when you abstain carnally from a man or a woman. A woman is a quart situation that where the template is not the same as yours and you do not project your mind away from the act while close to her, by the time you finish your spirit may die from your body and from that moment you cannot be in spirit for anything. However what **I AM** talking about has nothing to do with holiness or being powerful. Take for instance fire which can burn everywhere down but is it a **PEACEMAKER**? **I AM** talking about **PEACE** that calms every nerve and every situation and promotes **LOVE** and paves the way for **MERCY** to manifest and makes **KINDNESS** to work well and means that **RIGHTEOUSNESS** is revealed.

The Father of all potency is **PEACE**. Therefore, with this **FORERUNNER** of **PEACE**, the Kingdom has surely been established. **THE FATHER GOD'S** store is based on a **PEACEFUL** mind, a cold brain store and that is what I call King Solomon's Spiritual Library where all this information is kept for eternity. When I reveal these things such as this Lecture Revelation, you should listen and accept it if you wish, or if you do not like it then leave it but blessed are those who accept this information that has come this day in the name of our Lord Jesus the Christ, *Amen.*

SECTION THREE:
MIXED FORERUNNER

A **MIXED FORERUNNER** is a hint that something is coming, a sign of an oncoming occurrence. It is called a **HINT FORERUNNER**. The **HINT FORERUNNER** is **MY SPIRIT** in you when you become one with **THE FATHER GOD** by becoming **PEACEFUL** then I will indwell in you internally and I alert you when something is about to happen. For instance when some people hit their leg, either on the right or left they believe that it represents something. Therefore when this happens you will know what it stands for, as to whether it is a negative or a positive incident, according to your believe and that is a **HINT SIGN**

FORERUNNER. You may cut your tongue when you are eating and if you believe it, it is a sign that someone may be talking about you. There is a dream that when you have, it is a **HINT FORERUNNER** of an incoming event but if you pray over it then **THE FATHER GOD** can take it away because that event has not yet happened therefore, you stand a chance to bypass it. If you are in **SPIRIT** it means that, you are motivated in the consciousness of **THE FATHER GOD**, and you will be alert and know a **SIGN FORERUNNER** internally, which is what **THE FATHER GOD** operates. No one need give you vision because I can reveal things directly for you. For instance if you are going out and have forgotten your key, I can tell you that you have forgotten your key. I can go before you to show you that you have forgotten your key. **THE FATHER GOD** is the **FORERUNNER** of your physical life. **HE** will **HINT** you at every step so that you cannot make a mistake that will make you to cry. If someone wants to become your partner, I will tell you that you should do this or that because this person is not good and you will not be happy. So many things may take place as a warning before you involve yourself in that relationship. In the same vain, if you want to involve yourself in a financial matter and you are with **THE FATHER GOD**, I can tell you not to invest your money in that business because you will loose it. All these have nothing to do with vision or prophecy. I will tell you things face to face in you. I become **THE HINT** in you because in spirit, if you are a **PEACE PRACTITIONER** and a visionary, and you are a child of **GOD** then you and **THE FATHER GOD** become one. Your leg is **MY** leg therefore you do not have a leg again and you do not have hand again because I charge through out your body and superimpose and lead therefore whatever comes along I will take over and act. They will be seeing you but it will not be you. Evil people will see you but it is not you rather it would be **THE FATHER GOD** and that is why when you reach this stage, you have no problem again personally in your life. This is not a matter of collective action. It works for you and for your family, because before anything happens you will be there. Even your spirit or your word can countersign the event because you are in

THE FATHER GOD and **THE FATHER GOD** is in you. That is what I call the **SPIRITUAL FORERUNNER** and **THE HINT** before anything happens. You can only achieve this feet as a sign that you are a certified child of **GOD** when you have the ability see and weigh someone before you **LOVE** the person and know whether to be close or not as **THE FATHER GOD** will **HINT** you about that person. **I AM** telling you that this is the feet that you need to reach. Why should children of **GOD** should be taken unaware? If you are taken unaware in anything, it means that you do not tune yourself with **THE FATHER GOD** well, and you are not a **PEACEMAKER** because what is meant by **THE FATHER GOD**, is a **SPIRIT** that does not fear. **I AM EVERYWHERE**, **HERE** and **THERE**. It does not require church attendance or ministry work, **THE FATHER GOD** is in you twenty-four hours. **THE FATHER GOD** is in you operating non-stop, so with that you are secure. Do not play fool or joke with anybody that **I THE FATHER GOD** lives in even if it is a child of a day old. If **I THE FATHER GOD** is in anyone, he or she is greater than anybody in this world. He is more than any type of King. Whom **I THE FATHER** dwells with is prove that he or she is **THE FATHER GOD'S** child and **THE FATHER'S** son. Therefore, this is the attribute and the sign that you can use to know who **THE FATHER GOD'S** children are.

When you have **THE HOLY SPIRIT** in you that connect every positive attribute that proves you to be one with **THE FATHER GOD** then you can never make a mistake and know that anything that happens to you is by the architecture of **THE FATHER GOD**. And nothing can by pass **THE FATHER GOD** to do anything and even you cannot talk by your own fruition. Therefore if you understand this, then it means that you have no problem. Is it not true that when you sleep **I THE FATHER GOD'S HINT** is there and you will wake very quickly when any nonsense comes? **I THE FATHER GOD** can become the wing in you to fly away from rubbish. **I THE FATHER GOD** can become fire or anything of anything instantly in you when necessary because **I THE FATHER GOD AM ALL** and **ALL. MY** testing is **PEACE** and the other **FOUR STARS** in you and when I certify you with that then I will give you the approval that you are **THE FATHER GOD'S** son or daughter. Being **THE FATHER GOD'S** son, I live in you and you in **ME** then **WE** become one then all becomes well. Thereafter, your word will become honoured by **THE FATHER GOD**. When you speak, it is registered, and all spirits and angels carry out your instruction because it is not you that speaks, it is **THE FATHER** that speaks. That is why when our Lord Jesus Christ came to the earth as a **PEACEMAKER** with **LOVE**, he talked about **THE FATHER GOD** and promoted **THE FATHER** because he come from **THE FATHER GOD**. HE knew **THE FATHER GOD** therefore he and I **THE FATHER** become ONE and every utterance that he made, manifested because it was **MY** energy as **THE FATHER GOD** that operated through him. Therefore, today as I give HRM King Solomon David ETE the engineering of WORD, and make him a witness of the spoken WORD, **THE FATHER GOD'S** son and the Servant of the Lord, he is the mouth piece of '**AFTER THOSE DAYS SAID THE LORD**, **THE**

FATHER'S TALK (GOD PRESENT). That is why anything that King Solomon **ETE** *chop mouth* (says) about I honour it. How many people know that in this world whenever, Solomon ETE makes a pronouncement I honour it. He is the head of all Christ Servants. An 'Extraordinary World Wide Missionary Christ Servant' is his title.

I do not want to talk more about this. Let those who hear and listen to the **WORD** of **THE FATHER'S TALK (GOD PRESENT)** take the blessing of the day.

Song:
I AM THE PEACE, I AM PEACE blessed are the PEACE MAKER'S,
For they shall be called the children of God, blessed are the PEACEMAKER'S,
I AM THE PEACE, I AM PEACE blessed are the PEACE MAKER'S,
For they shall be called the children of God, blessed are the PEACEMAKER'S.

I AM THE PEACE, FATHER of PEACE blessed are the PEACE MAKER'S,

For they shall be called the children of God, blessed are the **PEACEMAKER'S**
I AM THE PEACE, I AM PEACE
blessed are the **PEACE MAKER'S**,
For they shall be called the children of God, blessed are the **PEACEMAKER'S**

Let **MY PEACE** and blessing abide with all **MY** children all over the world and Etteh Royal Universal family now and forevermore, *Amen.*

In the Name of Lord Jesus Christ
In the Blood of Lord Jesus Christ
Now and forever more

Thank You Father

Prayer by HRM Queen Disem Solomon David **ETE**

Let thanks and praises be given to **THE FATHER GOD** *in the name of our Lord Jesus Christ, Let thanks and praises be given to* **THE FATHER GOD** *in the blood of our Lord Jesus Christ, Let thanks and* praises be given to Leader **OLUMBA OLUMBA OBU, THE PEACE, THE SUPREME PEACE HIMSELF THE, ONE WITHOUT WHOM** there is no **PEACE** now and forever more, Amen.

Thank **YOU FATHER** for this Revelation Lecture about the **FORERUNNER** of all things, which **YOU** use to inform or warn your children about all pending events. Thank you for revealing **YOUR** personal **FORERUNNER** as **PEACE** and that without **PEACE** one cannot be **YOUR FORERUNNER**. Thank you **FATHER** that through this Revelation Lecture of the **FORERUNNER** you have made all your children **PEACEMAKER'S** and through that the ability to hear **YOUR HINT** and with that all is well with us now and forever more, Amen.

Let thanks and praises be given to **THE FATHER GOD** in the name of our Lord Jesus Christ, Let thanks and praises be given to **THE FATHER GOD** in the blood of our Lord Jesus Christ, Let thanks and praises be given Leader **OLUMBA OLUMBA OBU**, The Sole Spiritual Head of the Universe, Let thanks and praises be given to His Holiness, **OLUMBA OLUMBA**

OBU *and Let thanks and praises be given the Holy Mother* **OLUMBA OLUMBA OBU** *now and forever more, Amen.*

Ndito Akwa Ibom and A True Nigerian Man & Woman

PART FOUR

THE CHARACTER OF THE UNIVERSAL NEW WORLD

FATHER'S TALK
(GOD PRESENT)

Adam, Fifth James Father Two Thousand and Five (OE.OF.BOOE) Sunday, Fifth June Year Two Thousand and Five (05.06.2005)

In the Name of Our Lord Jesus Christ
In the Blood of Our Lord Jesus Christ
Now and forever more

THE CHARACTER OF THE UNIVERSAL NEW WORLD

(The Way Of Life Of The Children Of God On Earth)

Today is OE of OF of OE. And **I THE FATHER GOD** always comes to reveal one thing or the other that will help the new world to grow in perfection. Today I have come to reveal the character and manner of the universal new world. The title of today's Lecture Revelation is **THE CHARACTER OF THE UNIVERSAL NEW WORLD (THE WAY OF LIFE OF CHILDREN OF GOD ON EARTH).**

Everyone who lives on this earth plane and those who will come to live here will be having this as their code of conduct. This Code of Conduct of the New World Character is the behavioural stance **I** expect every human being on earth to adopt. This includes mode of inter-linking, interacting or what have you with one another. Failure to adopt this conduct is tantamount to not living on this planet. There is no joke any more.

First and foremost, I will talk about **LOVE** and other principles of **GOD'S** character which along with **LOVE** are **PATIENCE, HUMILITY, GOOD LIFE**, and **ONENESS**. These are the spiritual fruits of every human being as well as animals, fish and birds which are the four living creatures that represent **GOD**. They should have this character.

The new world bird should LOVE ONE ANOTHER. They should cooperate with all birds and human beings too. No birds should think evil or plan evil or try to harm another bird or human beings or animals or fish.

No animal should try to harm another animal or plan to harm any fish, bird or human beings. All animals should LOVE themselves and should practice ONENESS amongst them. Each animal should think of the welfare of a fellow animal, bird of fish. And they should not try to harm any human being. The same thing is applicable to fish. No fish should swallow each other. That is, the big fish should not swallow the small fish and the small fish should not eat the big fish. Every fish should LOVE, guide and protect other fishes. No fish should perpetrate evil against animals, birds or human beings.

Then human beings should love all human beings, protect human beings and think about the welfare of human beings like them. They should love animals, fish and birds. No human being should harm any animal, bird, fish or fellow human beings. This is the life of **THE UNIVERSAL NEW WORLD**.

THESE CHARACTERS WILL GENERATE IN THE ENTIRE NEW WORLD

The first **CHARACTER OF THE UNIVERSAL NEW WORLD** is **PEACE** through **LOVE**. Another character is

PATIENCE and another is MERCY; another quality is HUMILITY. GOODNESS is another character. Be good and practice goodness with everybody. All the four living creatures should think GOOD and SPEAK GOOD WORDS and practice GOODNESS. Exception of this, you will face judgement. Do you know what judgement is? The Law of Karma protects judgement and so whatsoever you put in, that you shall reap.

Divine LOVE is what every creation should practice. When you read the Lecture Revelation titled 'The Budget of the New World' you will come across this. I however, bring this one out in particular as **THE CHARACTER OF THE UNIVERSAL NEW WORLD**. Live and let live.

If you practice any incantations, do it for yourself. Do not let it touch another person. You are not even permitted to practice anything that is negative. You are required to practice LOVE. Therefore practice LOVE for another. You can practice PATIENCE with one another; you can practice love with one another; you can practice OBEDIENCE with one another; you can practice HONOUR and RESPECT with one another; you can practice MERCY with one another;

and you can practice **PEACE-MAKING** with one another. These are the characters that will generate in the entire new world, in spirit, in soul and physical reality, therefore, without these characters in you, forget about it because you are not amongst the light living souls.

When I speak like this, people think **I AM** joking but do not forget that in the beginning was the word and the word was with **GOD** and that word was **GOD**. Everything that you see and what you will see is created by the **WORD**. So when I speak as I do now knowing that **MY** words are positive that constitute creation. Do not think them as mere **WORDS**. They are registered in the order of G. O. D. This order is from **MYSELF OF MYSELF** and it must come to pass one way or the other and that is why **I AM TALKING, TALKING -TALKING, MAKING UTTERANCES THAT WILL NEVER FAIL**.

These are **HOLY** UTTERANCES OF THE SUPREME ENERGY, **THE FATHER'S TALK (GOD PRESENT)**. Whoever that gives a deaf ear to this destroys their soul. It does not matter who you are so far as you are one of the four living creatures, fish, bird, animal and human being you must obey the ordinance of **THE FATHER GOD THE CREATOR OF THE UNIVERSE** and **LOVE YE ONE ANOTHER**.

THE FATHER GOD in Adam is our Lord Jesus Christ was the ONE who promoted this law and **I THE FATHER GOD THE CREATOR OF THE UNIVERSE** have come to sanction it for eternity. The **LOVE** of **GOD** and man and all creations is **'love ye one another' - 'Live and let live'.** Think good thoughts, speak good words and do good acts. Additional requirements must include patience; must include humility; must include peace; must be long-sufferings attached to wisdom, understanding and goodwill and also power in good things.

BEHAVE AND IMPROVE TO SHARE IN FATHER'S KINGDOM

THE HOLY SPIRIT is the generator of the SUPREME POWER OF GOD that guides everybody wherever you are. **I AM** not permitting and have not permitted anybody to turn themselves into animals or fish or other things. You are not also permitted to turn yourself from fish to animal to destroy mankind. All the fishes that turned themselves to human beings should go back into the water, unless you come by the authority of **THE FATHER GOD** to improve your nature. If you come through **THE FATHER GOD** to improve your nature, then you should become a peacemaker and behave yourself. Do not corrupt the Human-Gods on earth.

For all fishes that came on earth to fornicate with human beings polluting them, and giving them the spirit of fish, making them to exhibit mannerisms of fornication that consequently destroy human beings, I have ordered them to return to fish and behave themselves as fish. Or they should **LOVE ONE ANOTHER** and improve to be human beings.

For all birds that turn themselves to human beings or allow human beings to use their souls in the darkness world to go about destroying people and destroying other lives, I have closed that chapter. I will return all birds to birds unless the birds practice **LOVE FOR ONE ANOTHER** and adopt the spirit of live and let live and they did not actually come to earth to destroy man or to be wicked to man. If you do not abide with the stipulated behaviour then all birds should go back to being birds. Then animals should stay in the animal kingdom or Queendom - whatsoever they call it. If animals turn themselves to become human beings or allow human beings to use their animal form to inflict wickedness on another human being then I thwart that practice. All animals that do not behave well are now returned to animal world. They should stay there and practice **LOVE FOR ANOTHER** or they wait for destruction.

It is only the ones who obey **THE FATHER GOD** and keep the instructions that will progress from animal to man, to serve man on earth. They are to serve Human-Gods on earth.

It is only the birds that harkens to this instruction, honour it and practice **LOVE FOR ONE ANOTHER** with dignity that will progress from bird world to human world and serve Human-Gods. It is only the fishes that keep these instructions that will progress from fish world to human world to serve Human-Gods. And all of them will share in **THE FATHER GOD'S** Kingdom because in **MY** Kingdom there are many mansions. This means that all the creations were created by **THE FATHER GOD** for the purpose of goodwill and coexistence.

Nonetheless, there are the stubborn ones that follow the spirit of Nothingness, the spirit of rebellion and revolt against the Divine Nature, the Divine Principle of '**LOVE ONE ANOTHER**' and good living and co-existence. If they still turn a deaf ear and rebel against this order, **I** will reduce them just like it happened to the serpent and the same thing will happen to all of them.

So today is the day **BY THE ORDER OF G. O .D** that **I DECREE THAT THIS SHALL TAKE PLACE IMMEDIATELY IN THE NATURE OF THE FOUR LIVING CREATURES**.

I AM THE DIVINE PRINCIPLE OF LIFE

The **UNIVERSAL NEW WORLD CHARACTER** is practiced by **THE FATHER GOD** and **HE** has infused these good characters into all the other positive children of **GOD** whether human-fish, human-birds or human-animals. However, the Human-Gods which are Man-Gods in the likeness of **THE FATHER GOD** shall rule over them for eternity. They shall be Kings and Queens under one King and one Queen, who are The Father and The Mother God respectively, on earth. This is applicable to all the planets.

So for this reason, from today onwards to eternity and for eternity this order shall exist. This order already exists in Heaven and must exist on earth. From the earth, it will spread over to the other planets of manifest, from the unseen to seen-able; unheard to hear-able and the not-touchable to touchable.

It pleases **ME, THE FATHER GOD** from the order of **MYSELF** to speak again on earth. *AFTER THOSE DAYS SAYS THE LORD IN THE DIVINE VOICE* of **THE**

FATHER'S TALK, (GOD PRESENT), I take this chance to explain **MY** immediate plan in the Advanced Life, so that everybody should behave well and be happy.

I emphatically elucidate the Practical Physical of the Human-Gods Life, which is the practice of physical living by the Human-Gods. Human-Gods are the Leaders and the Heads of all the other three creatures. Human-God in the woman (female) form will be the Mother and Human-God in man (male) form will be the Father. They are the Kings and Queens heading all departments of all forms of lives. They will be the overseers of all other creations. While these other creations serve them, they will be serving the **ALMIGHTY FATHER GOD** and **HIS** Christ, **THE KING OF KINGS AND THE LORD OF LORDS**. This is an **ORDER BY MYSELF IN MYSELF OF G. O. D.**

If any spirit, soul, angel, formula or object disobeys this order, I shall call that spirit, soul, formula or object to **MY** Hole and you expire for eternity. You will never surface again.

It has therefore pleased **ME**, The Divine Principle of Life because – **I AM** THE

DIVINE PRINCIPLE OF LIFE, to give **MY** principle of life to all **MY** creations, especially mankind. In **MY** Divine Principle of Life, I want peace on earth and in all lives. I want harmony and I want joy. I do not want lamentation. Do not be the cause in any manner, for anyone to cry or lament for **ME**. I will not take it kindly. That is when you will face judgement.

DANCE THE HEAVENLY EXPRESSION DANCE

I saw that human- beings were so low and so I pardoned mankind through the blood of Christ and I give man the opportunity to help themselves. This is the last chance. In this generation, I want peace; I want harmony; I want joy. Sing songs that honour **THE FATHER GOD**. Do not sing songs that honour evil.

All the evil practices on earth and all the rubbish dances shall cease to operate. Any dance done in the waist is a dance of fornication. When you see people dance in the waist, it is the snake dance - the dance of evil spirit, the dance of witchcraft. The dance in the waist represents serpent and it is evil because it is the dance of fornication. That generating energy of evil dance shall cease to exist. And those who dance in that manner shall face the consequences of their actions.

    The dance of the heavenly body is in the shoulder and hands with your body tingling with positive excitement with the sweetness of the heart and the mercy of **GOD** in you and the happiness and the flavour of the goodwill of **GOD**. It should include the sensation of **THE HOLY SPIRIT** around you and cause your body to tingle in a very nice and beautiful way, reducing you to smile with brightness on your face. That type of dance is the Heavenly expression. The dance of The Holy Spirit is the expression of thanking **THE FATHER GOD**. It is the expression of happiness, expression of truth, expression of oneness, expression of everlasting life and expression of the wisdom of The Holy Spirit. Consequently, you will be swimming in joy and you will be swimming in happiness. You will be swimming around, around and around with **THE FATHER GOD**, in the Atmosphere of Divine Dignity of **ME THE FATHER GOD**.

When you dance, you dance juju dance and fish dance. You dance animal dance. Are you animal? You are dancing fish dance- are you fish? You dance the bird dance – are you a bird? If you know that you are a Human-God representing **THE FATHER GOD** in a dignified manner, do not follow other people to dance these juju dances. What I mean by juju are all the elementary forces from the elementary creations. Fish is an elementary creation, bird is an elementary creation and animal is an elementary creation. It is only man that is the overseer of all these creations amongst the four living creatures. Therefore, when you dance, perform your dance to please **ME THE FATHER GOD** as an expression of joy; as an expression of happiness; as an expression of mercy; as an expression of peace and as an expression of all the fruits of the Holy Spirit. When these are expressed in you, it portrays the atmosphere of **GOD'S DIVINE PRINCIPLE**. Then that atmosphere spreads around people.

In contrast when you dance in the waist, shaking your body, your bottom and all that jiggling, dancing the dance of juju, you are spreading evil atmosphere. That is the dance Queen Sheba established in the juju throne. Are you then dancing the sort of dance that reveals your elementary form – jiggling your waist, bottom and all that?

So from today all the divine children of **GOD** should know the type of dance they perform. Dance the dance of good expression.

I USE THE SPOKEN WORD TO CONQUER ALL EVIL ON EARTH

The positive Human-Gods should know the type of communication and the type of business they establish. Anybody that establishes a brothel with its ill repute doing of keeping women and men to provide sexual services and also being involved with prostitution including the ones glossed over as escort services; instituting fornication and adultery outlets disguised as normal flats all reveal you to be evil. You will face the consequences of your actions.

You should not do anything to corrupt another person as you do not know whether they are from **GOD** from evil. You establish evil secret cults and destroy other people's good character through these and you also instigate children to be stubborn to their parents. If you share in the architect of these evil acts, I will hold you responsible and you will be destroyed a million fold.

I know what humankind is doing on earth through the evil instigation spirit soul. Evil has filled the earth. **MY SPIRIT** has also filled the earth. We are in the spiritual warfront now against evils and not human beings, but **I THE FATHER GOD** has conquered and I will conquer for all positive children of **GOD** for eternity because **I THE FATHER GOD** has the upper hand. **I AM THE CREATOR OF THE UNIVERSE**. I use the **SPOKEN WORD** today to conquer the whole evil on earth. And all **MY** divine children must not *follow-follow* and *borrow-borrow the evil ways of life*.

THE CHARACTER OF THE NEW WORLD requires you not to copy and or borrow ideas and things unnecessarily. If you do not know the origin of things and ideas then you cannot tell whether they are from the positive side of **ME, THE HOLY FATHER GOD OF ALL CREATIONS** as such do not follow or copy that character.

Anything that you join; anything that you copy; anything that you learn, anything that you borrow from any life at all, search and check and know the origin of that nature.

Do not follow any tradition. Do not say my parents' tradition; my father's tradition; my father's church; my mother's this or that or my parents' church. Do not follow anybody to any club. Before you follow anybody to anywhere or enter into anything check it first to know that what you are getting into is positive and established by **ME, THE FATHER GOD,** but of cause you will know things which are not positive.

Do not follow anybody to visionaries' and prayer houses. They are mostly disguised messengers of evil. They are the children of soothsayers. They are the children of Seers.

As they hear the name Jesus, Jesus proclaimed everywhere; they including native doctors also join to proclaim Jesus too. They call Jesus' name, and any name that strongly attaches to God, but they practice incantations. They have human skulls and use them for their nefarious activities. They pour wine on the heads of human beings and call on ghosts.

Elementary spirits operate under these people, but they pretend that they that they are calling **THE FATHER GOD**. They pretend they are worshipping **GOD THE FATHER**. They use Jesus name to operate; and they can even use OOO name. They can use any name but when you speak those names in your mouth and not from your heart they are not registered. Any word you utter, any idea you present and any pronouncements you make and the origin is not from **ME** then I will not sign them.

    This is **ME THE FATHER GOD** now coming with **MY** original ideas of the New World. What I want **MY** children to follow and what I want them to do. **MY** original idea of **MY DIVINE** principles of **MY** character is to **LOVE ONE ANOTHER**. Do not worship any idol. Do not believe in anything other than the **FATHER GOD, THE CREATOR OF THE UNIVERSE** and **THE CHRIST OF GOD,** through **THE UNIVERSAL SUPREME WORD**, which is **LOVE ONE ANOTHER**. If you believe the power of the **SPOKEN WORD**, make any pronouncement, make any utterance in any situation and leave it for **ME THE FATHER GOD**. Whatsoever happens afterwards is the will of **GOD**. Do not go anywhere else to look for any sort of help. Do not look for protection in any situation. Protect yourself in **ME THE FATHER GOD** through **THE NAME AND BLOOD OF OUR LORD JESUS CHRIST** as The Divine Protector.

PROMOTE ANYTHING THAT PROMOTES THE FATHER GOD THROUGH THE NAME AND BLOOD OF OUR LORD JESUS CHRIST

It has pleased **ME** today to speak **MY** mind and reveal the **DIVINE PRINCIPLE CHARACTER** that the children of **GOD** should adopt in the new world. Live and Let Live. Share what you have with people. Sponsor good and do not sponsor evil. Before you sponsor anybody check that the **DIVINE PRINCIPLE OF GOD LOVE** is there. Check that what you sponsor has the link to the divine will of **GOD** and that it has link with love. Also check that it is linked with peace and it has a link that leads to humility and it links and leads to mercy. Do not sponsor anything or any idea that will cause trouble or corruption which is likely to result in people deviating from **ME THE FATHER GOD.** If you do that you are evil and I count you as promoter of evil.

Sponsor LOVE; sponsor PEACE; sponsor PATIENCE and sponsor all good works. Promote anything that promotes **THE FATHER GOD**; that promotes the Energy of **GOD**; that promotes the Divine Principle of the Character of **THE FATHER GOD**. Do not promote anything that will not bring glory to **ME THE FATHER GOD**. If you do I will thwart you with your promotion.

In the whole universe discard all sorts of factions. Stay clear of them. Do not join any party, be it government, village, or any group or anything that you know to have been established before now to promote evil. Do not join them because if you do, you will be thwarted with that group and your evil ideas. Before now Satan and his agents had established so many cultures and so many, many traditions to imprison people and to enslave children of GOD.

Fish, birds and animals left their planets and invaded this earth plane. They take the form of human beings but their original templates are human-fish, human-birds and human-animals. They are here to try and improve themselves as I gave them the opportunity but they left the actual sense of improving themselves which was to worship **THE FATHER GOD**. They rather carved out ideas from their lower selves as **baby spirits** and use that to enslave the human-Gods. They brought laws upon laws and said that this culture is our culture; that is our tradition.

You that adhere to all these false establishments, have you asked whether that culture or tradition is from the **DIVINE PRINCIPLE OF THE CHARACTER OF THE FATHER GOD.** They say this culture is our culture – African tradition; *Oyibo* (white man) tradition; Chinese tradition, Indian tradition but all these traditions belong to evil. All these different areas have been previously captured by the heads of human-animals, human-birds and human-fishes. They worshipped dragons and all sorts of things before now. Nevertheless, I **THE FATHER GOD THE CREATOR OF THE UNIVERSE** has come to the earth to reveal **MYSELF** as The Human-God. The Divine Principle of **THE FATHER GOD** is to **LOVE ONE ANOTHER** and nothing but that. All the good characters come under that principle of **LOVE**, **ONENESS** and helping one another and the principle of knocking your head on the ground in any place holding the feet of **YOUR CREATOR** without anything like deathly Images talking to **ME** THE SUPREME SPIRIT OF ALLTHINGS through **THE NAME AND BLOOD OF OUR LORD JESUS CHRIST.** And that is the divine mode of worshiping **ME THE FATHER GOD.**

The earth you are walking on is the footstool of **THE FATHER GOD** while Heaven is the Temple of **THE FATHER GOD.** So if you turn your face upwards to Heaven, you speak to your **FATHER GOD.** If you bow down and look down to the earth, you worship in the feet of your **FATHER GOD.** That is all you should do and speak the word. Do not go to the tree; do not go to the dragon or the snake. Do not go the mountain. Do not go to all those places and do not do all those unrewarding things because if you do them you are promoting the idea of evil.

Speak to **ME** your **FATHER GOD** as you speak to yourself. Speak to **ME** your

FATHER GOD in the atmosphere of **THE HOLY SPIRIT OF THE FATHER GOD** - Everywhere, Here and There. Wherever you find yourself is **'GOD PRESENT'**. Wherever you are present as a Human-God **I, THE FATHER GOD, I AM** present in you there. That is what I mean by **'GOD PRESENT'**. Also whenever you are not there, **I AM** there for you in the soul or in the spirit. **I AM** Everywhere, Here and There. **I AM** in you here as **I AM** here now talking through King Solomon **ETE**, he is here with **ME**. When he is not here, **I AM** there with him. **I AM** everywhere with him. So wherever you are do not be afraid of anything - anything at all. Do not be afraid of those who turn to be birds and wear black cloths at night and fly and say that they will kill you. They have no power to kill anyone or destroy anything. I warned against that. They reckon Satan is powerful; *Oyibo* is powerful; *mami*-water is powerful; witchcraft is this and that – *who born dog!* Who gave birth to them to be powerful! Who gave them the power? Where do they exist from? I have made several explosives and I cause them to explode in any sanctuary or any place where there is darkness and the places there are the plans of evil. **MY** word shall stand for eternity.

So this is **MY VOICE – THE DIVINE VOICE OF THE FATHER'S TALK - GOD PRESENT,** today explaining **MY DIVINE CHARACTER FOR THE UNIVERSAL NEW WORLD** for eternity.

THE BODY OF CHRIST IS ALL FORMS OF FRUITS AND WATER IS THE BLOOD OF CHRIST

MY children are not authorized to *follow-follow*. Do not follow blindly. If somebody gives you a message and says it is from **ME THE FATHER GOD**, knock your head on the ground and pray to **ME** to reveal the actual source of that message. Do not allow anybody who is a witch or wizard and has planned evil in the witchcraft world to come back to tell you Father say this, Father say that and Father ask you to do this or to do that and sacrifice this or that. Do not allow anybody to deceive you in any such manner. **I THE FATHER GOD** has never asked anybody to sacrifice in water and to sacrifice anything to tree or to do anything as images or for you to do anything ritual in the night.

If they tell that **THE FATHER GOD** says do feast, that is an appropriate message. The feast **I THE FATHER GOD** requires is simple enough. It is to do fruit feast. Read and acquaint yourself with **THE FATHER'S TALK** Revelation Lecture titled '***THE FUEL OF HUMAN NATURE, THE BODY OF CHRIST'***. If you read this Lecture Revelation, you will know that I do not have any other communion and I do not have any other thing as the body of Christ. The BODY OF CHRIST IS ALL FORMS OF FRUITS that comes up from THE MOTHER Earth.

All the things that pop-up from the earth for instance rice, pineapple, pawpaw and all such things are the body of Christ. Who formed them? Is it not the SPOKEN WORD that forms them? For the Spoken Word said (YAK) *Let* be this and there was so. The SPOKEN WORD pronounced and it turned out to be all fruits, vegetables, seeds and all that is the body of Christ. What other body of Christ is greater than that? Is it the one *Oyibo* made? Is it the bread that they fry? Even biscuit is not in the least powerful compared to paw-paw, pineapple and banana.

Anything that pops up naturally from the ground and it is fruit, vegetable, herbs and a seed is the body of Christ. Also the pop up foods are as created by the SPOKEN WORD without the tampering and adulteration of any form or manner of man is the body of CHRIST. That is to say that, fruit and all natural living organisms in their divine nature is the body of Christ. Do you not know that water is Christ? The earth is Christ. Is it not the SPOKEN WORD that I used to create these things? And if these things become food and you eat them, they are curative. All the natural foods are medicines to cure all the infirmities in your system. Do you not see Soya beans? Do you not see paw-paw, orange, including all the leaves that you eat? They are all medicines for your system. They are the body of Christ and the water is the blood of Christ.

You see that is the significance of water that Christ used and said, 'drink this, it is My Blood and again He said eat this it is My Body. Now all fruits have been sanctified.

When you eat fruit, Satan cannot come closer to you. When you drink water Satan cannot get near you. Evil do not like water because it is the Blood of Christ. So the water represents the blood of Christ and the water came out from Him. And The SPOKEN WORD is Christ Himself. Then these words have become the paw-paw; become pineapple; become orange; become rice and other natural foods. When you bless all the things that pop-up from the ground and eat them, they become communion and you become one with **THE FATHER GOD** and one with Christ. That is enough. So if you do something else other than this it is a human ideology and your otherwise contra idea is not from **THE FATHER GOD.**

There is no borrowing in this Kingdom. **MY** CHARACTER is Divine. I do not borrow from any school; I have not borrowed and will not borrow from any situation. I do not borrow from anywhere. **MY** Character is Divine and from Heaven. Have you not heard the Revelation of John the Divine which the Spirit of our Lord Jesus Christ, as the spirit of love revealed?

I sent Jesus the Christ to send the message through John about the New Jerusalem which I will send down from heaven with new a name, consisting three names which are the name of **THE FATHER, THE NAME OF THE SON AND THE NAME OF THE HOLY GHOST**. They are the three capacities in the new name. Also the new name of the Kingdom, the New Jerusalem is not in the physical, it is in the spirit - everywhere, here and there. If you believe in that then you are in the New Jerusalem and the Spirit of Christ, **THE KING OF KINGS** will control you and rule as well as guide you. It is all in spirit! This Spiritual Kingdom is the best because wherever you are it stays with you. Wherever you are, you are with **THE KING OF KINGS AND THE LORD OF LORDS**. Wherever you are, you are with **THE FATHER GOD** and you are with **THE HOLY SPIRIT**. So tell **ME** what you will not to gain. It is only those who eat this hidden manner, this hidden wisdom and this Holy Spirit that will understand where they are. Have I introduced anything more than that?

IT IS ONLY NOW THAT PERFECTION HAS COME

Wear white. I say white garment to represent the righteous spirit, the divine goodwill spirit in you which is the Holy Spirit and to cover your nakedness. Any other thing is not of interest to **ME**. Reiterating - **I AM** not the least interested in any other thing but that you should wear white garments to represent the righteous spirit and to cover your nakedness.

I have come to establish the simplicity of **THE FATHER GOD** and the free goodwill for the new universe and that is what **I AM** backing. Anything that you do which is not authorized by **ME, THE FATHER GOD, I** will not back you therefore you will fail and when the consequences come, do not blame **ME**. So this **MY** Divine Principle **CHARACTER OF THE UNIVERSAL NEW WORLD** of the Divine Brotherhood of the Universe with man and **GOD** including the other three living creatures. It does matter because the four living creatures as man, animal, bird and fish are all brotherhood from the same Father but one should honour one. Fish, bird and animal should serve man as the Human-Gods. Man should serve Christ and Christ should serve **His FATHER, THE FATHER GOD** and everything should serve **THE FATHER GOD**. That is all. That is the order.

Everything you do must represent that order. Live in love, patience, humility, oneness, co-existence, joy, joy, joy, joy-y-y-y – joy! – For eternity! Allelu-u-u-u! Alleluia! Exception of these…well - well, well, well, you have yourself to blame. Do you think **I AM** not a leader? The leadership quality I have is both physical and spiritual and otherwise.

I AM the Leader to Unhearable and **I AM** the Leader to hear-able.

I AM the Leader to unseen-able; **I AM** the Leader to seen-able.

I AM the Leader to untouched-able and **I AM** the Leader to touchable.

So where will anybody bring an idea from which is from **ME** and I accept it. If you allow your child to direct you, you are accepting elementary directives because you are senior to your child. If you allow your student to teach you that means you are receiving elementary teachings because a student is lower than the master.

How can you be a master, or a tutor or a lecturer and you stand up to deliver a lecture, then one student will get up to direct you, making suggestions for you and correcting you? Then you as the lecturer accept such moves from the student and are happy to do so. How can you the lecturer happily accept such directives? That is ridiculous. This is what I have decided to reveal today.

So it has pleased the Holy Spirit that from today, everybody on earth will understand the meaning of **THE DIVINE PRINCIPLE CHARACTER OF THE UNIVERSAL NEW WORLD**. In this **DIVINE PRINCIPLE CHARACTER OF THE UNIVERSAL NEW WORLD,** I will not and do not accept any idea from any Master on earth. They are **MY** students. Every human being on earth is a student to this school. So I do not accept any idea from them. I do not accept any idea from any soul or spirit. It is only **THE SOLE SPIRITUAL HEAD OF THE UNIVERSE, THE FATHER GOD THE CREATOR OF THE UNIVERSE** that have the idea and plan as the master plan about the Kingdom as **THE UNIVERSAL NEW WORLD KINGDOM OF GOD**.

Therefore, be careful who you take directives from and who you copy from because everything from this world is from evil. It is only now that perfection has come. Okay, if those things were good why should **I, THE FATHER GOD** come? Why do I have to come now? Why should Jesus Christ say Father let thy kingdom come? So the Kingdom of Heaven will come and borrow from the kingdom of man? Man is looking for the Kingdom of Heaven so that what is done in heaven should be done on earth. Is it not so? If therefore man is waiting for that why should I come from Heaven to borrow human ideas? Stupidity! Ignorant! I thwart that! I hate that!

I rebuke that concept! – Now and forever more! Amen!

Let **MY** peace and blessing remain with the entire world now and forever more. Amen.

In the Name of Our Lord Jesus Christ
In the Blood of Our Lord Jesus Christ
Now and forever more

THANK YOU FATHER

PART FIVE

THE VOICE OF THE CREATOR

Ndito Akwa Ibom and A True Nigerian Man & Woman

Father's Talk
(God Present)

Enoch, Sixteenth James, FATHER Two Thousand and Eight (AF.OF.OH)   (Monday, Sixteenth June, Year Two Thousand and Eight (16.06.2008))

In the Name of Our Lord Jesus Christ, In the Blood of Our Lord Jesus Christ, Now and forever more

THE VOICE OF THE CREATOR OF THE UNIVERSE

THE FATHER GOD ALMIGHTY TO ALL HUMAN BEINGS ON EARTH

This is the **VOICE OF THE CREATOR OF THE UNIVERSE THE FATHER GOD ALMIGHTY** to all human beings on earth. *This is the final information and the last remedy to solve the universal Problems of mankind: natural disasters, sicknesses, and conflicts, wars between nations, disagreements, and the reporting of many incidents* *of death and general destruction on earth.*

A: **I, THE FATHER GOD THE CREATOR OF THE UNIVERSE** deserves recognition and total acknowledgement as **THE SUPREME FATHER** who creates and owns all spirits, souls, angels, humans and everything created seen and unseen

B: All **MY** creations should have the total belief in **ME THE SUPREME FATHER GOD THE CREATOR OF THE UNIVERSE**, and refrain completely from worshipping of idols, elementary spirits of any kind, practicing wickedness of any form, and disassociate completely from any negativism and incantations.

C: Everyone should join His Royal Majesty King Solomon David Jesse **ETE**, the original incarnate of Abel, the positive son of Adam and Eve to celebrate and appreciate **ME, THE SUPREME FATHER GOD ALMIGHTY**, through the universal programme of the **UNIVERSAL SUPREME WORD SEASON CELEBRATION**, which is a yearly event.

I AM THE UNIVERSAL SUPREME WORD, the **MOTIVATOR** of **LIFE** and **LIGHT** of **LIFE SUPREME ENERGY**. Therefore, any living soul that rejects this order has himself or herself to blame because of the universal testing programme that **I AM** going to start, in spirit, soul and physical, to shake the world, to remove all shakeable things away, and leave all the positive things to remain on earth.

It has pleased **ME, THE FATHER GOD THE CREATOR OF THE UNIVERSE** to have long patience, the longest of all long patience's up to this time. All negative human beings, negative Kings and Queens, negative Heads of States, negative Presidents, negative Governors and negative, daughters and sons of all human beings give deaf ears to **ME** and **MY WORD OF LOVE**, and all the preaching **I** have been passing through **MY** positive Servants to deliver. They still treat the world as though it belongs to them with total power of evil maintaining that there is nothing like **THE FATHER GOD THE OWNER OF THE UNIVERSE**.

The whole world has refused to acknowledge **MY** presence as the

SUPREME WORD, THE SUPREME SPIRIT, and the Owner of ALL things. They rather worship negativism. They worship mermaids and elementary spirit-souls instead of their **CREATOR** and as a result, **I** have no other option than to exercise **MY** Ownership on earth in whatsoever form **I** like from now on.

So, what human beings will see on earth from now onwards, starting from a very limited time (and nobody should predict time for **ME**), they should not doubt.

Nobody knows **MY** will. **I** will do what **I** want and select the positive and destroy all negatives in spirit, soul and physical present. Therefore, in spirit and in the soul, if you give a deaf ear to this information then, **I** repeat, you have yourself to blame and your soul and your blood will be upon you.

I do everything to salvage humankind and to save your soul, because **I** know the problem you will face if your soul falls into darkness hell. It is so severe. Everlasting punishment is so severe, which **I** do not wish any of **MY** creations to face. That is why being that **I AM LOVE, I** always bring a remedy to humankind in the time like this on earth. So, this is the last and the final remedy through **THE VOICE OF THE CREATOR** to you all **MY** creations.

What was done in Heaven should be done on earth, which was the pleading of the higher positive spirit soul of Adam, which is our Lord Jesus Christ that, what happened in Heaven should also occur here on earth. So, now this is what will happen here on earth:

Every soul and every human being will join to celebrate ***THE UNIVERSAL SUPREME WORD SEASON*** and recognize **THE FATHER GOD** in all aspects of life and shun all negativism. Without that well…! This is your last chance.

THE UNIVERSAL SUPREME WORD SEASON CELEBRATION covers the following celebration criteria and appreciations –

A: Celebrate and appreciate **THE FATHER GOD THE CREATOR OF THE UNIVERSE**

B: Celebrate and appreciate the first human beings Adam and Eve, our first Father and Mother, the universal Parents of all human beings (BROTHERHOOD) on earth

C: Celebrate and appreciate the positive life – our lives on earth.

D: Celebrate and appreciate **THE FATHER GOD.** The divine breathe of life in you – your personal life.

E: Celebrate and appreciate **THE FATHER GOD** the soul of life in you as your personal soul.

F: Celebrate and appreciate **THE FATHER GOD** for sound health in your human physical presence here on earth.

G: Celebrate and appreciate **THE FATHER GOD** for **HIS** love, peace, mercy, kindness, equality, goodwill, righteousness, joy and happiness, long life and prosperity and the rest of all **HIS** good countless goodness for humankind.

H: Celebrate and appreciate **THE FATHER GOD** for **HIS** positive **DIVINE SELF, THE HOLY SPIRIT OF TRUTH, HE** is the **SPIRIT** of all things **BROTHERHOOD**

I: Celebrate and appreciate **THE FATHER GOD, HIS** Divine positive soul, **HE** is the **WORD**, the Supreme Word of the Universe.

AO: Celebrate and appreciate **THE FATHER GOD**, for **HIS** Positive Divine Power, the Holy Spirit of Truth personified on Earth.

THE CELEBRANT- EVERY HUMAN BEING IS A CELEBRANT

The above are the reasons that every human being is a celebrant of <u>***THE UNIVERSAL SUPREME WORD SEASON CELEBRATION***</u>. Therefore, it is a must and compulsory that every living soul, especially humankind should participate in this programme with all their heart.

This is the only way **I, THE FATHER GOD THE UNIVERSAL SUPREME WORD, THE CREATOR OF THE UNIVERSE** will give you credit that you recognize **MY EXISTENT AS THE FATHER GOD ALMIGHTY YOUR CREATOR**.

Nevertheless, this can only be done if you **LOVE ONE ANOTHER** and appreciate another life like life in you. Also you appreciate **ME THE FATHER GOD**, **THE SUPREME WORD** that lives in every soul by respecting and valuing another life as all life and all living creatures.

Let **MY** peace and blessing abide with the entire world, now and forever more. Amen.

In the Name of Our Lord Jesus Christ, In the Blood of Our Lord Jesus Christ, Now and forever more

THANK YOU FATHER.

Ndito Akwa Ibom and A True Nigerian Man & Woman

CHAPTER SIX
THE INSPIRATIONAL WRITER

Ndito Akwa Ibom and A True Nigerian Man & Woman

KING SOLOMON SPIRITUAL LIBRARY
THE GOD ENCYCLOPAEDIA WORD OF INFINITY

INSPIRATIONAL WRITERS AND READERS OF THE
FATHER'S TALK
(GOD PRESENT)
KING SOLOMON SPIRITUAL LIBRARY

In the name of our Lord Jesus Christ In the blood of our Lord Jesus Christ Now and forever more, Amen

(A) REFERENCING THE FATHER'S TALK (GOD PRESENT) IN KING SOLOMON SPIRITUAL LIBRARY

I know some people will inspire when you visit King Solomon Spiritual Library website or bookshop, and have access to any of **THE FATHER'S TALK (GOD PRESENT)** information through books, electronics, audio and otherwise and are inspired to write or produce any information through the knowledge that you have gained, you must not fail to reference **THE FATHER'S TALK (GOD PRESENT) in King Solomon Spiritual Library** as the such of your inspirations.

(B) THE WORD OF TRUTH AND THE HOLY SPIRIT PRINCIPLES

Since **THE FATHER'S TALK (GOD PRESENT)** is the direct information from **THE FATHER GOD ALMIGHTY HIMSELF,** all positive children of God can be, and will be inspired with this

WORD because the Word of **THE FATHER GOD, THE CREATOR OF THE UNIVERSE** is a Spiritual Case Study for all souls to improve to have self awareness and a Higherself Consciousness.

When you are inspired and you want to write, make sure that your ideas, principles and concepts base on the Holy Spirit of Truth without changing the ordinance of the **FATHER'S TALK (GOD PRESENT).**

(C) THERE SHALL BE CONSEQUENCES THAT WOULD FOLLOW THOSE WHO USE THE MEANING, THE CONCEPTS AND THE PRINCIPLES OF THE FATHER'S TALK (GOD PRESENT) FOR THE PURPOSES OF MISLEADING

Consequences shall follow those who use the meaning, the concepts and the principles of **THE FATHER'S**

TALK (GOD PRESENT) for the purposes of misleading in any manner.

Any Human-God, human-animal, human-bird or human-fish who has access to **THE FATHER'S TALK (GOD PRESENT)** through any means, be it via books, electronics, audio and otherwise should know that those words are not the words of human beings. The words are transcribed, proofread and accepted by **THE FATHER GOD** as it comes from the **SUPREME STUDIO OF THE ALMIGHTY FATHER GOD HIMSELF,** via **King Solomon Spiritual Library.**

When the signal of the information alerts HRM King Solomon David Jesse Etteh from **THE FATHER** through the **COMPREHENSIVE MEMORY OF GOD** in him, at anytime in the day or at night and anywhere, whether on the road or any public place, he will take note of the title of the Revelation Lectures. Sometimes if the location is conducive, lectures can take place immediately. If the location is not conducive, **THE FATHER** fixes the time for the full lecture to take place. Most of the time, some of the lectures take about a week, a month or six months and so on, to deliver when **THE FATHER** brings it back from **HIS SUPREME MEMORY** to HRM King Solomon Etteh.

Take note that the information of **THE FATHER'S TALK (GOD PRESENT)** is not preaching, or the giving of sermons or shared discussion. **THE FATHER** calls it "***LECTURE REVELATION***", which is a Spiritual Case Study for mankind to improve and have the Higherself Consciousness about himself or herself and their creator.

For that reason, every human being that comes across any of this information of the **FATHER'S TALK (GOD PRESENT)** should treat it with utmost and absolute respect and reverence at all times.

HRM King Solomon David Jesse Etteh is not responsible for **THE FATHER'S TALK (GOD PRESENT)** but **GOD HIMSELF. THE ALMIGHTY FATHER** only uses him as a way through, just like a loud speaker from the radio or television receiver.

For this reason, HRM King Solomon David Jesse Etteh will not be held responsible by anyone who does not understand the contents, the concepts and the principles of **THE FATHER'S TALK (GOD PRESENT)** information in King Solomon Spiritual Library. He will not answer any questions or queries from spirit to soul and the physical truth in connection to the above from the lower mind individuals, persons or groups. However, if you are positive and you have love, you are humble, have patience and are peaceful and you want to know and understand more of any part of **THE FATHER'S**

TALK (GOD PRESENT); 'You should use fasting and prayer' and or if anyone has any questions in good faith, he or she is free to write to HRM King Solomon and **THE FATHER** in him will respond. He will not, and there is no response to any questions, queries and anything negative with the craftiness of the evil minds of humankind.

That is why you should first read

THE FATHER GOD with **HIS SUPREME HOLY SPIRIT OF TRUTH** will bless all those who read and accept this information with good faith through the name and blood of our Lord Jesus Christ. Amen.

In the name of our Lord Jesus Christ In the blood of our Lord Jesus Christ Now and forever more, Amen

"THEUNISAL-SUREME SEACELION"
The Universal Supreme Season Celebration
=========
"THEUNI-SUREME WORA THECRO-THEUNISE"
The Universal Supreme Word Almighty
The Creator Of The Universe
====================
WWW.COME4WORD.COM

THE OFFICIAL SITE FOR

=============

EVERLASTING UNIVERSAL ALL WORD

Ndito Akwa Ibom and A True Nigerian Man & Woman

SEASON APPRECIATION CEREMONIAL PROGRAM

==========

THE UNIVERSAL SUPREME
ALL WORD
SEASON

Ndito Akwa Ibom and A True Nigerian Man & Woman

CELEBRATION
(GOD PRESENT)
SOMETHING MORE THAN
GOLD
IN THE HEART OF ALL MEN IS THE
WORD

====================
THE WORD IS THE MAKER, THE SOLE ADMINISTRATOR AND THE CREATOR OF THE UNIVERSE.
THEREFORE, ALL MANKIND ON EARTH MUST APPRECIATE THE WORD IN ALL CAPACITIES FOREVER
================

FROM EVERY OA OF AO TO AO OF AO (1st OCTOBER TO 10th OCTOBER.) YEARLY IS THE UNIVERSAL SUPREME

ALL WORD SEASON

CELEBRATION TO APPRECIATE THE FATHER GOD ALMIGHTY

Ndito Akwa Ibom and A True Nigerian Man & Woman

WORDWORDWWORDWORDWORDWORD

CELEBRATION!
CELEBRATION!!
CELEBRATION!!!

THE UNIVERSAL SUPREME **WORD** CELEBRATION OF ALL TIME

Ndito Akwa Ibom and A True Nigerian Man & Woman

THE ALMIGHTY FATHER GOD, THE CREATOR OF ALL THINGS BROTHERHOOD

ORGANISED BY KING SOLOMON SPIRITUAL LIBRARY

======

HRM KING SOLOMON DAVID JESSE ETE
INSPIRATIONAL HEAD

IN THE HONOUR OF THE FATHER GOD THE CREATOR OF THE UNIVERSE THE HOLY SPIRIT OF TRUTH AND THE KING OF KINGS AND THE LORD OF LORDS

==========

THANK YOU FATHERo

Ndito Akwa Ibom and A True Nigerian Man & Woman

KING SOLOMON SPIRITUAL LIBRARY

THE GOD ENCYCLOPAEDIA WORD OF INFINITY

==========

King Solomon Spiritual Library, God Universal Information Centre Father's Talk (God Present)

WITH LOVE

Covered: This **BOOK,** e-book, software or software's, books, website, video, audio, idea or ideas, formula or formulas, manual or instruction manual.

... Hereby gives you a non-exclusive license to use the ... (THIS BOOK). Some of the word here is coded with the (WORD OF SUPER HOLY AND INTELLIGENCE FATHER GOD ALMIGHTY)

Title, ownership rights, and intellectual property rights in and to the Website, Books, E-book, Audios and Videos, Shops and Store – e-Stores, Fundraisings, Celebrations and the supreme word seasons Celebration formulas and arrangement, Positive Inspiration, Holy (Fata), FATHER GOD ALMIGHTY POSSESSING SPIRIT in thought, in words and in did, thinking well, speaking well, hearing well and doing well shall remain in me and in ... The BOOK is protected by international copyright.

FATHER'S TALK (GOD PRESENT)

The message in The Father's Talk (GOD PRESENT) does not challenge any authority either individuals, groups or governments of any land or even any belief of any form. It is rather challenging the truth that is hidden from mankind. Therefore, any spirit, soul or physical human being who decides to challenge this truth shall have himself or herself to blame.

Key A
Any individual that reads any of The Father's Talk (GOD PRESENT) with faith; love and acceptance will experience immediate positive change in his or her life from spirit, soul to physical. If he or she accepts the message then he or she will be free from any evil.

Key B: **PEACE AND LOVE**
If you do not believe the contents of any of The Father's Talk (GOD PRESENT) it is possible through The

Father's divine love and peace simply hands over your copy to a friend or somebody else that would like to keep a copy, or signing out from any of the website that connected to The Father's Talk (GOD PRESENT) KING SOLOMON SPIRITUAL e-LIBRARY without any evil and negative comments and you are blessed and free.

========

FROM THE DESK OF INSPIRATIONAL HEAD

Fees, Prices and Donations; There is no refund on fees, price or donations since your fees price or donations are using as a charity contribution to do administration work of THE SUPREME WORD, So please kindly read this first before you decide to involves yourself in any of the under mention of HRM King Solomon David Jesse ETE universal Inspirational Businesses of (GOD PRESENT) in cash, kinds and otherwise.

I CAME FROM THE FATHER GOD, WITH THE FATHER GOD, AND BY THE FATHER GOD TO ESTABLISH THE FOLLOWING:
Therefore, all distributors and contributors of The Father's Talk (GOD PRESENT), The Spiritual Advice, Healing and Counselling on General Live (The Universal Supreme Spiritual General Hospital), New Songs and Psalms of King David and Solomon, The Word of **GOD** Processing City in Ikot Okwo or e-City online, The Trinity Celebration, "**OUC FUND**", The Universal Bank Account For All Creations, "**ERUFA**" ETE Royal Universal Family, "**THEUNISAL-SUREME SEACELION**" The Universal Supreme Word Season Celebration To Appreciates THE FATHER GOD ALMIGHTY "**THEUNI-SUREME WORA THECRO-THEUNISE**" The Universal Supreme Word Almighty, THE CREATOR OF THE UNIVERSE should attach this information to all

readers, website visitors, distributors, affiliates person/group, celebrant and celebrations centres, supporters and promoters, members, workers and voluntary workers, Ete royal universal palace committee, governments and many other centres as an agreement. Please kindly know that I am not answering to any physical human except **PEACE, UNITY AND LOVE.**

"**THEUNISAL-SUREME WORA THECRO-THEUNISE**".

I AM IN THE STAGE OF SUPER HOLY AND INTELLIGENCE FATHER GOD POSITIVE MADNESS OF THE HOLY SPIRIT OF TRUTH, ENYEN ODUDU ODUDU ODUDU ABASI MI OOO ZIM ZIM ZIM ASSASU, POSITIVE POSITIVE POSITIVE. UKEMEKE AKA IDIOK UNAM.
Let the peace and blessing of the Holy Father abide with everybody who

corporate with this divine Father's Talk (GOD PRESENT

THANK YOU FATHER

BY
THE HOLY SPIRIT OF
THE FATHER GOD
THROUGH HIS SERVANT
Senior Christ Servant
HRM King Solomon David Jesse ETE
Brotherhood of the
Cross and STAR
Eteroyal Universal family
Ikot Okwo The Great City of Refuge,
Ete Community
Ikot Abasi LGA-543001
Akwa Ibom State Nigeria-W/A
Tel. 08036693841
www.ksslibrary.com
Email: ksslibrary@eteroyalmail.com

READ AT LEAST SEVEN LECTURE'S REVELATIONS BEFORE YOU CAN MAKE ANY COMMENTS

In the Name of Our Lord Jesus Christ In the Blood of Our Lord Jesus Christ
Now and forever more

Everybody should have access and read at least seven **FATHER'S TALK (GOD PRESENT)** Lecture's Revelations before you can make any comments about it. If you do not go through at least seven **FATHER'S TALK** lectures and you comment you may make mistakes. When you make mistakes your blood will be upon you because you would have taken voluntary evolution to misquote **THE FATHER GOD THE CREATOR OF THE UNIVERSE.** If however, you go

through any seven of **THE FATHER'S TALK (GOD PRESENT)** –
one of **THE FATHER'S TALK** stands for one Spirit of God, which means that **FATHER'S TALK GOD PRESENT** Lectures Revelation are witness by the Seven Spirits of God, which **I** use as the Seven Church of God and Seven days of the Week, Seven spirits of Creations in one Supreme energy of THE FATHER GOD, THE SPOKEN WORD.
When you read seven **FATHER'S TALK L**ectures then, **I THE FATHER GOD** will reveal you as positive person. Then you will have a portion in **ME**. One of **THE FATHER'S TALK** will have a portion in you. Then you would know that this information came from **THE FATHER GOD.**
The Father's Talk God Present is not a mere talk from a man!
In the Name of Our Lord Jesus Christ In the Blood of Our Lord Jesus Christ

Now and forever more
WWW.THEWORDCITY.COM

www.ksslibrary.com

THE UNIVERSAL SUPREME ACKNOWLEDGEMENT

'THE ONLY SOURCE AND REMEDY
TO END ALL HUMANITIES PROBLEMS'

Join me to Celebrate;
Acknowledge,
Appreciates and give full
RECOGNITION to
THE UNIVERSAL
SUPREME WORD,
YOUR LIFE FORCE,

Ndito Akwa Ibom and A True Nigerian Man & Woman

THE TOTALITY OF ALL TOTALITIES YOUR CREATOR, THE FATHER GOD ALMIGHTY, THE CREATOR OF THE UNIVERSE

WWW.COME4WORD.COM
Contact EMAIL:
hrmkingsolomon@eteroyalmail.com

THANK YOU FATHER

ESTABLISH MY SPIRITUAL LIBRARY

I THE FATHER GOD ALMIGHTY THE SUPREME WORD OF THE UNIVERSE AM THE SPIRITUAL FOOD TO FEED YOUR SOUL. Therefore, **I** want every family in this world, every home in this world, every office, government offices, monarchies, countries, states, regions, counties, communities, local authorities compound, family homes, everyone everywhere should be collecting published copies of **THE EVERLASTING GOSPEL AND THE FATHER'S TALK (GOD PRESENT)** Lectures Revelations of KING SOLOMON SPIRITUAL LIBRARY should be established physically in your houses. So that everybody should have those RECORDS. Go to read the books regularly. Every family should have this Library **MY**

INFORMATION CENTRE for their family members.

Every generation of the particular family could easily go to their family Library of **KING SOLOMON SPIRITUAL LIBRARY EVERLASTING GOSPEL** and the **FATHER'S TALK (GOD PRESENT) Lectures Revelations** and read the Gospels and Lectures Revelations. Generations upon generations will access their KING SOLOMON SPIRITUAL LIBRARY.

You must all have **THE LIBRARY OF THE FATHER GOD ALMIGHTY** called **KING SOLOMON SPIRITUAL LIBRARY FATHER'S TALK (GOD PRESENT) LECTURES REVELATIONS** in your homes and offices. The authorities and individuals concerned must see to that. When you establish your branch of KING SOLOMON SPIRITUAL LIBRARY and have Everlasting Gospels and the **FATHER'S TALK (GOD PRESENT)** Lectures Revelations that place is blessed and secured. In the name and Blood of Our Lord Jesus Christ, now and forever more, Amen.

THANK YOU FATHER

The title List of some of the

Father's Talk
(GOD Present)

1: THE MANUAL OF THE SPOKEN WORD

2: THE MANUAL OF LIFE

3: INVESTMENT WITH GOD

4: ISO IBOT EDEM IBOT

5: THE CHARACTER OF THE NEW WORLD

6: HELPMANTRANS

7: UNDERSTANDING MY WORD

8: TRUTH, POSITION, POST AND NAME

9: NON STOP BLESSING

10: IMPRESSION

11: STAGES OF EDUCATIONS (SPE, SSE & SUE)

12: THE ENGINEERING OF LIFE

13: THE CONTENT PACKAGE

14: THE BUDGET OF THE NEW WORLD

15: DIVINE ATTENTION

16: THE BABY SPIRIT

17: PROMOTION

18: ADVANCE AND PROGRESSING MIND

19: THE TEMPLE OF THE LIVING GOD

20: I AM OK

21: THE SPIRIT OF TRUTH

22: THE PERFECT PERMANENCY

23: THE FATHER GOD, GOD, GOD THE FATHER

24: HUSBAND, WIFE AND CHILD

25: GOD AND HIS HARBINGER

26: LIFE EVERLASTING

27: POSSESS

28: MY MIND AND MY PLAN

29: AFTER HEART AND AFTER MIND

30: MY DECLARATION & STAND IN BCS

31: BEYOND THE HOPE OF FAITH

32: MENTAL STAIN

33: THE PRINCIPLE OF SELF HOLD

34: THE MASTERSHIP

35: HIDU-CUM

36: THE UNIVERSAL PARENT

37: ADVANCED YOU AND ME

38: THE GREAT UNIVERSAL CHANGE

39: THE PROJECTED MIND
40: INDESTRUCTIBLE BLESSED FIVE STARS

41: ASTROTS, GOD PRESENT I AND MY FATHER

42: SONGS THE COMPLETION

43: THE RIGHT BUTTON

44: AKWA ABASI IBOM- ETE - DIRECTING NDITO AKWA IBOM

45: THE DIGITAL AGE

46: GOD IS OFFICIAL CHAMPION

47: A TRUE WITNESS

48: MYSTERY OF PROCREATION AND BIRTH

49: THE UNIVERSAL UMBRELLA

50: **THE FORERUNNER**

51: A OF A TO Z (FIRST OF ALL)

52: MAN IN THREE CAPACITIES

53: THE TRUE LIFE OF HOLY SPIRIT PERSONIFIED

54: IN-BETWEEN THE FATHER & THE SON

55: DIVINE ARRANGEMENT & AUTHORITY

56: TWENTY FIRST CENTURY IS NOT FOR SATAN

57: THE SUPREME WORD SEASON CELEBRATION

58: THE MAXIMUM DEITY

59: TRANSFORMER TRANSMITTER AND WAVE

60: THE SUPREME FUTURE

61: THE BYLOVE OF WORD

62: THE SIGNATURE OF THE FATHER GOD

63: THE TWO WAYS

64: THE UNDERSTANDING OF LIFE

65: THE GREATER THAN SOLOMON IS HERE

66: THE CONQUEROR

67: THE SPIRITUAL GENERAL INSPECTOR OF LIFE

68: THE NIGERIA IN THE AFRICA Part one

69: THE NIGERIA IN THE AFRICA Part two

70: THE CREATOR AND CREATIONS PART ONE

71: THE CREATOR AND CREATIONS PART TWO

72: THE CREATOR AND CREATIONS PART THREE

73: THE SUPREME TEACHER

74: THE SPIRITUAL COVER

75: THE NIGERIA IN THE AFRICA PART THREE

76: THE SUPREME BELIEVE

77: CAST AND BAN (LECTURE IN LIVERPOOL)

78: LIFE EXTENSION MANUAL

79: THE SPIRITUAL TRAFFIC

80: <u>THE VOICE OF THE CREATOR</u>

81: MY OFFICE

82: LIFE SPIRITUAL FIRE EXTINGUISHER

83: INFORMATION

84: FATHER GOD FINAL ARRANGEMENT

85: THE LOVERS OF CHRIST

86: I LOVE YOU, I LOVE YOU TOO

87: THE UNIVERSAL SUPREME UPDATE

88: THE SUPREME ALTAR

89: THE SOURCE AND DESTINATION

90: A SON LIKE THE FATHER THE KING OF KINGS A ROOTS FROM HEAVEN (NOT THIS TIME AROUND)

91: THE TRUE WITNESS AND THE TRUE SERVANT

92: THE FINAL ARRANGEMENT

93: <u>A TRUE NIGERIAN MAN AND WOMAN</u>

94: EVERYONE MUST PERSONALLY INVOLVE

95: BEWARE

96: ESIEN EMANA AKPAN "THE AFRICAN PROBLEMS"

97: THE SECRET OF THE UNIVERSAL PROBLEMS AND THE REMEDY (MUSLIM AND CHRISTIAN FROM THE SAME PARENT)

98: MMU-UDIM – THE BLESSED MOTHER (ABASI ME UDIM)

99: THINK WELL, SPEAK WELL AND DO WELL

100: THE STAGES OF HOW TO PROCESS THE WORD

101: EVIL STAIN, WHO RUNS AWAY FROM WHO

102: BEYOND HUMAN KNOW PURELY SPIRITUAL

103: <u>THE INSPIRATIONAL WRITER</u>

104: BIAKPAN OBIO AKPAN ABASI (THE NEW JERUSALEM CITY)

105: "OBAMA" THE STRAINTHEN AND THE SPIRIT OF BILL GATE AND MICROSOFT

THANK YOU FATHER

www.ingramcontent.com/pod-product-compliance
Ingram Content Group UK Ltd.
Pitfield, Milton Keynes, MK11 3LW, UK
UKHW041257180426
11947UKWH00008B/523